Dear Heather.
might be

LETTERS TO MY SISTER

Tales of the Old Brynna

lots 4 love

John Hiett
23.2.21

JOHN HIETT

LETTERS TO MY SISTER
TALES OF THE OLD BRYNNA

Published by Magic Flute Publishing Ltd. 2021

ISBN 978-1-909054-73-8

Magic Flute Publishing Limited

231 Swanwick Lane

Southampton SO31 7GT

www.magicflutepublications.co.uk

A catalogue description of this book is available from the British Library

Contents

The Author

John Hiett was born and bred in the Brynna. At 16 he started as a coal miner, and at the age of 24 became manager of a coal mine in Somerset. After ten years of managing coal mines, and with coal mines closing all around him, he moved to NCB headquarters in London to take charge of practical training for graduate mining engineers. Five years later he set up a conference and exhibition company to organise events all over the world, from Monte Carlo to New Orleans, Berlin to Hong Kong, Singapore to Paris, New York to Dubai. He also started a music company, putting on 15 concerts in the Royal Albert Hall. In his spare time he organised an annual Watch and Clock Fair.

He spent 17 happy years managing the conference business at the University of Southampton, and on retirement interfered with life in his home village of Titchfield Hampshire.

At the age of 85 he started a new career in writing. Working from his 15th century home, this is his third book.

Acknowledgements

This series of stories started as letters to my sister Anne, to amuse her during the Covid crisis of 2020. Anne encouraged me to continue, copied the stories to my fan base and persuaded me to publish. If you like the book, tell me; if you don' like it blame Anne.

Every author needs a publisher, and my publisher is Bryan Dunleavy of Magic Flute Publishing Ltd. He knows all the things about publishing which I don't, so my grateful thanks go to Bryan.

Every author needs someone to bounce ideas off, and for that I thank Lorraine Finch. I not only bounced ideas off her, I gained ideas for stories from her chatter. Lorraine is also my proof reader so any mistakes are hers not mine.

And finally there is my sister Wendy, my Welsh agent and IT specialist.

The Prussian in the village

The day war broke out was a beautiful sunny September day. All was right with the world. I was racing down Southall Street on the pavement opposite our house on my single roller skate. I couldn't afford a pair. Our maternal grandfather came out of his house, next door to ours, and came towards me. He gave me threepence. It was the first and last money he ever gave me, but I understood. He was living on just the ten bob a week Lloyd George pension then.

He told me that we were at war with Germany, and, no doubt because I was his eldest grandson, he told me the secret he had held for so long. He was afraid that he would be arrested and interred for the duration of the war.

He had a strange accent, and he had told us that it was because he was from the Forest of Dean. Not a bit of it. He was a Prussian. He had been a cavalry officer in a Prussian Cavalry regiment stationed in Lens in France. Everyone, of course behaved with Teutonic courtesy - except for one officer, a German named Mann who had somehow been accepted into the regiment.

Our grandfather was in love with a countess who lived in a sort of castle in the town, and Mann deliberately insulted her. Grandfather demanded satisfaction and Mann agreed to a duel at dawn. Mann produced a box with two pistols. Grandad choose one, Mann took the other. The two seconds marked out the distance and the Colonel, very reluctantly, gave the order to March, turn, fire.

Grandad was the best shot in the regiment and fired first

- and missed. Mann jeered at him, asked him to apologise to save his life. Grandad said "fire when you are ready" and stood proudly to his full height of five foot.

Mann fired and then announced that he had not put bullets in either pistol. The Colonel was so appalled by this churlish behaviour that he dismissed Mann from the regiment on the spot. Mann climbed into the saddle and galloped off towards the town.

In the town the countess saw Mann galloping past her window, assumed the worst and fell into a faint from which she never recovered. When grandad went to see her she was breathing her last.

He left the regiment and came to England, assumed the name of Thomas Evans, married Rosie Fields and came to work in Brynna Wood Colliery. His secret was safe with me, until now. He was never arrested. But you will remember that sometimes he looked as if he were in a trance. That was when he was remembering Lens, the countess and Herr Mann, who ruined his life.

Could this be Tommy Evans? A miner undercutting coal in his stall, in a thin seam, lit by a solitary candle.

The Pig Incident

The Spanish Civil War attracted a lot of young British men to Spain to fight in the International Brigade for the working man against General Franco. It was a badge of honour. No-Good-Boyo was a devil-may-care handsome vagabond who came back from the war in the late thirties along with Will Paynter. Will Paynter went on to become President of the South Wales Federation of Mineworkers. I met him many years later when he was a distinguished old man. He looked and behaved like an Old Testament prophet. He remembered No-Good-Boyo with affection. No-Good -Boyo never amounted to anything.

His careless attitude to life and his playboy aspirations meant that he couldn't get a job of any sort. Out of pity, and to get him off the Parish books, the Parish offered him a job cleaning the road gutters in Brynna.

Nobody wanted to give him a room in Brynna, so he moved up to the Huts, at that time the poorest part of a not very prosperous village. We were only just beginning to get over the Great Depression.

That was when he got his first bit of luck. A woman living in the Huts with her teenage daughter fell hopelessly in love with him. Her name was Dawn, but she was known as the Wolf Woman. I used her character in a book I published in 2018. It was a story set in the year 1670. I described her in the book as follows:

> "She was past her prime, but tall and lean still. Beneath her thick red hair her face was pale,

but in that pallor two great eyes, their beauty enhanced by a dark veiled glow - and lips so fresh and ruddy they seemed to devour you alive. She had about her that look which is peculiar to women who are desperate to be loved. They called her the Wolf Woman because she was never satisfied"

She set her hat at No-Good-Boyo, but he laughed at her. "Why should I take the cow when I can have the heifer?" He said. She was so besotted that she invited him into her home, even gave up her bedroom for him, which he shared with the daughter while she slept in the kitchen, huddled up to the ashes in the grate.

She still pursued him, even though her daughter, now in love with Boyo, called her names, and said she would report Dawn to the police. "Do that and I'll kill you" her mother said.

The more he refused her the more she wanted him. She worked in the fields. She was as strong as any man, and wherever Boyo worked she followed him. He complained to Mr Davies the Chapel Superintendent who said that he'd pray for him. He reported her to the policeman in William Street who said Dawn has committed no crime.

One day, when he was back at his old job cleaning the gutters, the pig incident happened. You will recall that the houses in Brynna had a fire downstairs but upstairs was always cold. Some people kept a pig upstairs to provide a bit of warmth, and one of these pigs jumped out of the window and fell on No-Good-Boyo. He was rushed to hospital, close to death, It was thought he wouldn't survive, but he pulled through.

As soon as he was on his feet she was after him again.

They grew corn on the mountain at that time, up past Mr Perry's house. The corn grew to six feet in height. No-Good-Boyo got a job cutting the corn with a scythe. She went up there, filling her apron with blackberries for him. He told her that if she didn't leave him alone he'd swing for her. Next day she was there again, picking wimberries I knew this because I had followed her up there, both days, out of sight and watched as the drama unfolded. No-Good-Boyo was having a doze. She ate some wimberries and kissed him with her lips tasting of wimberries. This time he didn't turn her away. He succumbed. She closed her eyes slowly, like a wolf does, like a woman who doesn't want to see what is being done to her body.

When it was all over he seemed to realise what he'd done. He screamed at her, "You witch, I'm going to kill you". She said, "Kill me if you like. I can't live without you"

I saw the flash of the sun on the blade of the scythe as he raised it. I turned and ran down the mountain. I don't know what happened. They might have run away together, or he might have killed her, buried her body and run away himself. Nobody knows, and nobody cared, because the next day war was declared, and we had other things to worry about.

Above: Southall Street, Brynna. Apart from the cars, little has changed since the 1930s.
Below: St. Peter's Church.

The American Boys

Brynna wasn't exactly at the centre of operations in World War II. But we did have an anti-aircraft battery in Brynna Wood. A small number of soldiers had a searchlight and a gun. They had a quiet war. We made friends with one of the soldiers, Alan Burgess, from Fulham I think. He was well over six feet tall and felt faint when he bent over. He used to come for meals with us, and we remained friendly even after the war.

There was also an American contingent camping at St Mary's Hill. We called them all Yanks. We boys would walk up there. "Got any gum, chum?" They gave us what they called candy, even odd cigarettes, and some people of a certain gender got nylon stockings. Old Mrs Roberts in William Street managed to get a pair. She wouldn't wear them. She was keeping them for her funeral.

She wanted to meet her God in nylon stockings.

The Yanks were always friendly and courteous. Far from home and waiting to go to France they didn't come to the village much. But there were two young soldiers, Hank and Chuck, farm boys from the Great Plains. They had never left the State, let alone the USA before they were called up. They were both 18 years old, still mother's boys.

They felt quite at home in the wide and verdant Vale of Glamorgan. On their day off they used to walk down to the village, follow Church Street to the Mill. The road bridge crossed the river there and they would tickle a couple of trout and fill their water bottles. Then they would walk up to Ty

Charles Farm, which was a few cattle, a few horses, including a magnificent hunter on which I had ridden, and a lot of sheep. They would light a fire, cook the trout, lie in the sun and walk back the way they had come. They missed their families, of course, but were very happy with life.

Ty Charles was farmed by two brothers and their sister Marie. Marie was plump and jolly. She must have been about the same age as their mothers back in the US of A. After a while Marie made friends with the boys, talked farming with them, let them help a bit. She would give them a pail of milk to drink. An affinity grew between the two boys and Marie.

But it wasn't the same affinity for both boys, and Marie became aware of this. Chuck saw her as a substitute mother, Hank as something else. The two boys had been inseparable, but now she easily persuaded Chuck to look after an

injured sheep while she and Hank went into the woods to look for another lost sheep. They came back some time later without a sheep but with Hank wearing a smug look on his face.

The next week Hank went off early from the camp without taking Chuck with him, and returned late that evening. Chuck challenged him and Hank confessed that he had been to Ty Charles alone.

The next leave day Chuck was up early, and the two went up to Ty Charles.

Marie rushed out and was disconcerted to see Chuck there. The three walked to the edge of the woods, and Marie made an excuse to go into the woods with Hank.

Chuck was very quiet on the walk home. Hank couldn't get a word out of him.

When they got to the mill Chuck climbed on to the rails

of the bridge and gazed into the river. He leaned over and Hank was alarmed. "Have a care, Chuck" he called, "you'll fall in". As Hank watched Chuck leaned further over the rail and very slowly fell over it into the water.

They found his body further downstream the next day. Another casualty of war.

The American CO held an inquiry. He questioned Hank who said that he had no idea how Chuck had fallen into the water.

It was all hushed up!

What happened to
Meidryn Owen's sister

The Square in Brynna was dominated by the Eagle pub. It sat at the corner of Southall Street (where we lived, which ran northwards) and Church Street, which ran West. There was an unpaved lane running from Church Street behind the Southall Street houses. Where the lane reached our house there was a spur running along the backs of the Church Street houses. The lane was used for collecting the ashes by horse and cart every day. Mrs Owen lived in the first house in Church street after the Lane. So her outside toilet at the end of her back garden was very near to our outside toilet at the end of our back garden. So we could talk to each other. She lived with her son Meidryn who was a little younger than me and her daughter Betty who was a few years older than me.

Betty, who was a very pretty teenager, suddenly disappeared. "Gone to London" said Meidryn. We boys knew what that meant. Meidryn said she had gone to join a circus. She just disappeared. Nothing was seen of her again for forty years, when out of the blue she introduced herself to me.

I was working then at the University of Southampton, running the conference business. I was marketing the facilities - lecture theatres, bedrooms, catering etc in the vacations to those who wanted to run conferences and meetings. A nun named Sister Maria was coming to see me. When she came into my office I noticed that she was walking awkwardly. I wondered whether under that Nun's habit she had a wooden leg, and if so, how she had lost it and how much of it she had lost. She looked to be in her late fifties. Perhaps she had been in London during the war. She had a really beautiful face. The phrase "remnants of a great beauty " came into my mind, but it was more than that. She was beautiful still. There was a sadness about her, which I put down to the pain in her leg.

Her first words to me were, "You're John Hiett aren't you. From the Brynna. I'm Betty Owen."

To say that I was dumbfounded would be an understatement. My mind flew back to when I had last seen her. I would have been about 12.

I stuttered and sputtered and tried to bring the conversation back to her conference needs. I asked her whether I should call her Sister.

Maria or Maria or even Betty Owen. She said I should call her Sister Maria. But I confess I was consumed with curiosity about what had happened to her after she left the Brynna. This is what she told me.

The Nun's story

When she went to London she didn't join a circus or go on the streets. Quite the reverse. She became a nurse at the Hospital for Tropical Diseases. She was "specialling" a young chap, an army captain who had returned from Burma with a nasty ailment (no, not that one), His life was in the balance, but Betty and her colleagues looked after him so well that he eventually pulled through. As often happens, nurse and patient fell in love. Before he was discharged he invited Betty to come to his home in Norfolk for a weekend to meet his mother.

Betty wanted to take a present for his mother, but she had so little money left from her wages as a student nurse, after paying for her board and lodge at the Nurses' Home that she couldn't afford much. So she painstakingly made her some tatting, in the Brynna fashion, with his mother's initial (A for Anne) tatted into the pattern. She wrapped it in crepe paper and put it into a nice envelope.

She loved the train journey over the flat countryside. The train clattered over the rail joints, saying "see you soon, see you soon, see you soon". She leaned back on the moquette seats. She couldn't have been more happy. She could never have imagined a Brynna girl becoming the chatelaine of a country house in Norfolk.

She took a taxi from the station. "Start as you mean to go on," she said to herself. There was a gate in the wall surrounding the estate and a long yellow drive through parkland to get to the house. It stood behind a gravelled area where the taxi pulled up. The main part of the house was old brick, two storeys tall. At the side was a tower and attached to that a modern extension, one storey only, more glass than wall, and all white. She could see a swimming pool inside.

A butler came out of the arched entrance and took her little cardboard suitcase. He took her into the library where Anne and another woman sat at tea. They were graciously welcoming. Anne introduced herself and her sister Bunty, James' aunt. She was offered tea and Battenburg cake, and then Anne suggested that she might be tired after the journey, and need a little rest before dinner. "We eat at seven" she said, and rang the bell for the butler. It was all like a dream for Betty.

Caruthers the butler took Betty to the tower. On the top floor the stairs opened into a large square bedroom. On one wall was a fireplace; the stairs were on one side of the fireplace and on the other side was a bathroom. The other three walls had large mullioned windows looking out over the rolling parkland of the estate. Betty lay on the bed and relaxed in bliss. She was warm and comfortable.

It was almost dark when she awoke, nearly seven o'clock. She quickly tidied herself up and went down to the main house for dinner.

Anne and Bunty were perfect hosts. They made Betty feel at home, asking her about her job, and how she liked it, and saying how grateful they were for looking after James. Anne had actually heard about Brynna!

Between the fish course and the main course there was a subtle change of tone. Bunty took over the conversation.

"Did you have a nice rest in your room? Did you manage to sleep?"

"Yes I did. It's a lovely room. But something rather odd happened"

"Oh indeed. What was that?"

Betty said "I don't know if I dreamed it. It seemed so real at the time. I thought I woke up and saw an old lady outlined against one of the windows"

"Tell me" said Bunty, "what did she look like?"

"She was quite tall, slim, dressed in black in an old fashioned sort of way. Her hair was grey and was worn up on top of her head. Eerie. Do you have a ghost in the house?" She laughed.

Bunty hesitated, took a sip of wine. "What happened next, my dear?"

"She didn't say anything, but she beckoned to me and I took a few steps towards her until she raised her hand to stop me. Then she just looked at me and shook her head. The next thing I knew was waking up in bed. It must have been my imagination"

"Are you sure she shook her head?" asked Bunty

"Oh, I'm sure about that; I just don't know what it means"

Anne took over the conversation. "My dear, this family has always been a matriarchal society. That's strange, because the eldest son succeeds to the estate, marries a woman from another family and that woman takes control of matters. It was the same two hundred years ago, when there were two grown sons in the family. Both were engaged to be married. The two young ladies were brought to the house, as you were and as I was, and taken to see the old grandmother, who was still ruling the roost. She was confined to bed in the tower, where you slept. She beckoned each girl in turn to come towards her. For one she nodded, for the other she shook her head. The one she approved of was allowed to marry her fiance, the other one was sent away.

Since that time, every prospective bride has been sent to that room. All saw the old lady as you did. It happened to me. I got the nod." She paused and leaned forward. "We both like you very much Betty. We can understand why James fell in love with you. But you will understand that he can't marry you."

The next morning Betty came downstairs for breakfast. Only Caruthers was there. He served her breakfast and called her a taxi. He was very sympathetic. He felt her pain.

As the taxi drove away Betty looked out of the back window. James was standing in the archway. He was weeping.

I never did find out if she had a wooden leg.

The Momentous Day of the Apple

The 11 Plus led me to Bridgend Grammar School for boys, considered to be the best Grammar school in Glamorgan, and I was in the express stream. I had to give up wood work for Latin and Art for something more deserving, like another science.

The Western Welsh bus took half an hour or so to get to Bridgend. I used to get off by a pub near where my Granny Hiett lived, and walk up the hill to the school. Going home, I had to walk to the other end of town to the bus station, and stand in a queue (a gwt we used to call it). The bus was always full by the time it reached the bus stop where I got off in the morning, so, I wouldn't have been able to get on. We were confined in a snaking railings in the gwt like sheep waiting for slaughter. Schoolboys rarely got a seat. It was standing all the way home, even if you had a bad foot.

For some reason, possibly because the bus started its journey to Bridgend at Llanharan, only a mile from the Brynna, there were always seats available on the morning journey,

The buses had a driver's cab separate from the bus interior, and at one time during the war the buses were converted to gas rather than petrol. There was a big rubber gas bag on top of the bus. An ideal target for German fighter planes, I thought.

The other change the war brought was that we had a bus conductress rather than a conductor. On that momentous morning of the apple I saw an empty seat in the front row. There was a fat bloke sitting on the inside seat. He had a mac folded across his lap. I sat next to him.

There was a blower leading from the driver's cab, and a fan blew hot air from the engine into the body of the bus. The conductress was standing with her bum against the fan. She was wearing a utility skirt. "Utility" was a war time fashion. Clothes were cut to use the minimum amount of cloth consistent with maintaining decency for the wearer. Her utility skirt, which came down to the middle of her knee caps, was fluttering in the breeze from the fan. She wasn't very old and was obviously unused to being at work. The fat bloke next to me was in a state of excitement. He wanted to talk to her, but hadn't been introduced.

His face was flushed, and before we passed the finger post he exploded with excitement. He had decided to use me, a poor schoolboy, as his intermediary. His hand was underneath the mac on his lap. Without warning, he flung the mac aside, and there in his hand was a big red apple. He passed it to me to give it to her. She blushed prettily and demurred. She couldn't possibly take a gift from a stranger, particularly a PASSENGER.

So there was I, in this electrically charged atmosphere, holding in my hand this symbol of original sin, and feeling for the first time in my life that delicious flutter in my groin.

My thoughts turned to Miss Morgan. Mine was a Boys' Grammar School, with only men teachers. But in war time they were hard to find. So we had this one woman, Miss Morgan. She was tall and elegant. She looked French. She had dark hair piled on top of her head and wore bright red lipstick on her generous mouth. She, too, wore utility skirts. When she sat on the radiator at the front of the class her skirt would ride up to the top of her softly moulded knee caps in their glittering nylon stockings. She knew the effect she was having on us boys. We were goggle-eyed.

So I didn't give the apple back to the fat bloke. I determined I would give it to Miss Morgan, and so win her favour. But by the time I got to Bridgend the feeling had passed and I ate it. When I got home Mam said to me, "What did you learn in school today?"

The Poor Old Man

There is a lot of contention in our family about who fetched the milk. I think I fetched it from the time I could walk until I started work down the pit, and then my siblings took over. That's why I know so well the way from our house to the farm from which I fetched the milk, and why I was leading the procession going to the Christmas party for customers at Will and Marie King's farm. It was on the outskirts of the Brynna, perhaps half a mile from our house. So it was a long way for a little kid on a winter's morning, before a crumb of breakfast.

On the evening of the Christmas party there was quite a crowd going down the road. I was running ahead, then running back to the group to make sure they were following me. Dad was talking to Mr McAndrews, who was a Public Speaker and used long words like "pnuemoconiosis". Mam was in some sort of women's' guild and was talking to other women about something which went over my head. Joe was in the pram. He was about two. Margaret was pushing the pram. It was a Silver Cross pram. Marg wasn't very pleased either. She couldn't see over the top of it, and had to find her way by peering around the side.

When we reached the farm there was a fire roaring in all the downstairs rooms. The children were put in one room to watch a magic lantern show, slides showing black people without many clothes, brought back from Africa by missionaries. I have to say that the technology was interesting but not the subject matter, which wasn't helped by Mr Davies mixing up his notes while he talked about the slides. Before long we had abandoned Mr Davies, who ploughed bravely on, and we wandered into the parlour, where the grown-ups were talking, eating and drinking.

They were also doing turns. That girl of Underhill with the big chest was playing the accordion, punctuated by occasional gasps, while an old chap accompanied her on the spoons. I jumped in with a Limerick.

> There was a young man from Siberia
>
> As a father was rather inferior
>
> But one operation
>
> With one permutation
>
> And he was a Mother Superior

Someone shouted "I heard that on the wireless" and Mr McAndrew muttered under his breath "Plagiarist". I was only four, and thought that a bit strong. If I'd known how to spell it I'd have looked it up in my "Collins Dictionary for Brighter Boys" which Mam had bought me for my fourth birthday. Turns out it wasn't the last time I was given that appellation.

Dad had a nice tenor voice, and he was being pressed to sing "Give us a song, Law" they cried. He demurred, as always, but then stood and braced himself to sing. At that moment the door burst open. Icy air poured in, along with No-Good-Boyo, with a long overcoat flapping around his ankles. He was wearing a hat with a piece of elastic going under his chin to hold it on. He had just returned from Spain and felt the cold.

"There's a man down, by the finger post" he shouted.

We all trooped out of the house, leaving Margaret to look after Joe, who was grizzling, again.

Outside it was bright as day. Millions of stars were pressing down on us. It was bitterly cold. The ruts cut up by the cattle in the field had frozen solid. I felt I could strike sparks off the ruts with my hobnailed boots. We walked hurriedly to the road and down the lane towards the finger post.

The old man was lying on the verge. He was a big old man with a beard and wearing lots of ragged clothes. He was lying on his back, one hand underneath him. The other hand was at his side, palm upwards, fingers just curled as if he were trying to catch raindrops. His finger nails were long but remarkably clean. His chest was large and still.

The men had a little committee meeting. There was a brief discussion about whether they should move him a little distance into the next Parish, but that was quickly discounted.

Will King, known affectionately as King Billy, offered to keep the old man in his barn until the next morning, when the coroner could be informed. Two men went back to the farm to bring a door to carry him on. While they were gone there was talk about who he could be. Nobody had seen him before, and it was concluded that he was a tramp.

He took a bit of moving, onto the door, and they agreed which four men should carry him first, and which others should take over the burden. It was quite a steep climb from the finger post to the road.

Someone suggested there ought to be a prayer. Mr McAndrew said " Dear Lord, accept our prayer in Thy righteous wrath". I thought, "righteous wrath? I haven't done anything wrong. I don't deserve wrath, righteous or not". It seemed that most of the people there thought that Mr McAndrew was on the wrong track, because they turned to Mam, whose sole qualification for leading a prayer meeting was that she cleaned the brass in the chapel. I could see a tear frozen on her cheek bone.

She stepped up to the mark. "Dear Lord" she said, " Take this poor man into one of your many mansions and let him be warm. Amen"

The Secret Savant of the Brynna

I had lost my frog. I wandered down the lane at the back of Church Street looking for it. I didn't see the frog, but I saw Mr Milligan leaning on his gate. He hadn't seen my frog, but he invited me in to see his postcards. They were in full colour, and, in monochrome war-time Britain the cards were a revelation. He showed me a picture of the Taj Mahal, and explained its story; he showed me a picture of Ayers Rock in Australia and told me the geology. He was a man of great equanimity, and his explanations were wonderfully explicit.

I told Dad about him, and he told me that Mr Milligan was a scab, a blackleg. He had continued working in the strike of 1926 and he and his wife had been "sent to Coventry". No-one spoke to him or about him, and twenty years later that still applied. I think Dad felt that the embargo should have been lifted long ago, but the code of the mine-workers, like the Omertà of the Mafia, was unrelenting. Dad seemed quite pleased that I was talking to him, bringing some relief into his lonely life.

But his life was far from lonely. He had pen-pals all over the world. He used the very simple fact that people liked receiving nice letters. They appreciated that someone had taken the trouble to put pen to paper and write to them personally. But Mr Milligan made an art of it. He never presumed to offer advice; he was deferential without being obsequious; he had the wonderful gift of being able to delineate the elements of a problem so that the recipients of his letters could decide on what action to take.

He and his French wife Clemence had no children. He spoke to her in French, in which he was fluent. Since no-one spoke to the couple she didn't have the chance to improve her English, so she was pleased to practice on me.

He had made a lot of beautifully polished wooden trays, connected together on one wall, which he used as a filing system.

He told me that to ensure people read his letters he only used beautiful paper and envelopes and had a selection of papers in his trays. No ruled feint Basildon Bond for him. He also had a collection of fountain pens and he would chose paper, and pen and ink colour which he thought would suit the person he was writing to. He wrote to people who he thought needed a shoulder to cry on, people he thought he might be able to help. Other trays held letters he had received in reply to his.

He persuaded me not to reveal to others what he was doing. He didn't want people to think him presumptuous. He searched among the trays to find some letters he had received which I might think interesting.

He showed me a letter from the King, on Buckingham Palace headed notepaper. It was hand-written, and began, "Dear Milligan. Thank you for your letter of 26th ult.". It was signed "George R".

In it the king expressed his thanks. He said that Mr Milligan had confirmed for him just how much his staying in the UK meant to his people in England and the Empire, and to the soldiers risking their lives for their country. He had decided that he and the Queen and the two princesses would stay in England "until victory is ours". I believe he had been under some pressure from his Privy Council to at least send the Princesses to safety in Canada.

There was a letter too from Winston Churchill. He addressed him as "Dear David". His particular reason for writing was to tell Mr Milligan that one phrase David had written "Never has so much been owed by so many to so few," had struck him to the heart, and if Mr Milligan didn't mind he would use it in a speech later that week. We, Mr Milligan and I, had the pleasure of listening to a recording of that speech on the wireless at the end of the war, and we exchanged a quiet smirk.

Mr Milligan had been writing to troubled people ever since he had been "sent to Coventry." There was quite a lot of correspondence between him and Frederick Delius the composer in the early 1930s. Delius' father, a prominent Northern businessman had wanted him to go into the family business, but Frederick bravely defied him. He wanted to be a musician and consequently struggled all his life.

He was never rich, and for the last six years of his life was blind and partly paralysed. It was a desperate time. He found a young man named Eric Fenby, himself an accomplished musician, who became his amanuensis. Eric went to live with Delius and his wife Jelko, so Delius could continue to compose music, which Fenby committed to paper.

Mr Milligan wrote to Delius in 1930 and showed me the reply, written by Fenby, who said that Delius was much moved by the letter. Mr Milligan continued to write to Delius until his death in 1934, using a special ink he had made up by adding chalk to it, so that when it dried (never blotted) the ink was raised. He used full foolscap paper and large writing so that the old man was able to read it by touch.

Strangely enough, I met Eric Fenby many years later at a function. He was a quiet old man, and introduced himself to me as "I am Eric Fenby. I was Delius' amanuensis". It was a significant moment for me. Doesn't life keep coming around to remind you?

I asked Mr Milligan if he'd had any disappointments. He sighed and said "I've always believed that it always works out for the best in the end. And if you believe that, John, really believe it, it will work out for you like that. But my letter to the Shah of Persia turned out to be the exception that proved the rule"

The Shah of Persia had been shoe-horned into the job by the Americans and the Brits in 1941. They were wanting to protect the oil supply. Persia (now Iran) was more like a Western state than a Middle East state. Like the Lebanon, it was a playground for the rich. There were fine hotels, restaurants, ballet, theatre, all the good things of life. But the Shah was profligate. He and his wife Farah threw huge parties, spent enormous sums of money, and the people, particularly the religious people, were becoming restive. Mr Milligan wrote to him and received a reply written by a Grand Vizier "His Serene Highness has asked me to reply to your kind letter...."

"Whenever you get a letter like that, John" he said, "you know that the person you wrote to never saw it. Some flunkey decided it wasn't important enough to bother the Shah with. I fear not only for the Shah but for the whole Middle East"

The Shah lasted until 1979, when the revolution came and Iran turned into a theocracy. The Shah and his wife and five children were exiled to Egypt where the Shah mysteriously died in 1980. His daughter Leila poisoned herself and his son, a student at Harvard, shot himself. I often wonder how different affairs in the Middle East might be today if only the shah had read Mr Milligan's letter.

H.M King Zog of Albania ruled with his Queen Geraldine from 1928 to 1939. At that point he decided it would be safer if he went into exile in England. They lived modestly in Maidenhead. In 1944 Enver Hoxha became the communist leader in Albania and King Zog realised that he would never regain his throne.

Mr Milligan decided he needed a letter so he wrote to him. King Zog replied saying:

> " How prescient of you. You are right. It does always work out for the best in the end. All these years I have been worrying about my kingdom. Now that worry is all over. I can live a peaceful life. I am moving to the Cotswolds where I will be unknown, and where I have bought a small farm. My new kingdom is bounded by hedges. My new perfumes include the scent of hay. I am a contented man. Thank you.
>
> Yours sincerely, for the last time,
>
> Zog"

Hoxha unleashed a reign of terror in Albania; we only found the depth of it when he died in 1985. At this time I was living in Titchfield, and an alcoholic friend of mine named John, a journalist and yachting correspondent for the Daily Telegraph was living with his alcoholic wife in The Long House near the Bugle. John was writing a book about Hoxha. As soon as he finished it Hoxha died and no publisher would touch it. You can expose a tyrant who is alive, but not a dead one, apparently.

It was only a couple of months after D Day. Things were going pretty well at the front when I popped down to see Mr Milligan. He was deep in thought. "I have to write a letter to Senator Joseph Kennedy" he said. Senator Kennedy was not a particularly well-liked man, and I wondered why he had been chosen for a letter. He and his wife Rose (who lived to be 104) had nine children. Of that nine four died violently.

The youngest and last of that benighted family, Jean, died in June 2020

Their oldest boy, Joseph 11 had been killed in action in the Pacific. Their son Jack (later President) had been shot down but survived. Their daughter Kathleen, described as a "socialite" had become Marchioness of Huntingdon in 1944, but her marriage lasted only four months. Her husband was killed in action in Belgium. Hence the letter to the Senator.

"Do you think he'll reply." I asked. "I do hope so," said Mr Milligan, "there's a lot of bleakness in his life at the moment, and, I fear, more to come."

He chose a pale cream paper, and the ink in his fountain pen was more violet than blue. The words flowed like cream over the paper, serene and warm. After 76 years I can't remember exactly what it said, and I hope you will forgive my poor attempt to paraphrase it; it was something on the lines of:

> "I know you have suffered great tragedy in your life, and that you sometimes despair. But I also know that sometimes, when you walk through the woods into a shaft of sunlight, or when a grandchild looks to you for help, you feel a spark of life, a little moment of wonder. You see that it's your choice, the life you lead is up to you."

The Senator did reply, a month later. He sounded very humble for a senator. He really needed a friend who asked nothing of him.

Tragedy followed the Kennedy family like an avenging angel. Kathleen, only four years after becoming a widow, was killed in a plane crash when she was on her way to a holiday in the South of France with her married lover, the 8th Earl Fitzwilliam. His son Jack (the President) was assassinated as was his son Bobby (the Attorney-General) and his son Ted left a girl to drown when he drove his car off the road into a creek in Chappaquiddick. Strangely enough, that incident brought me into second-hand contact with the Kennedy family forty years after my first encounter.

Ted's wife Elizabeth, broken by her husband's infidelities, had gone off the rails and become a drunk. She was saved by a friend of mine, a pain doctor in Boston named Gerry Oromof. Gerry was a speaker for me at a conference I organised in London on pain treatment. One of the rules for his success was that he would only accept patients who WANTED to be freed from pain. Some people enjoy the attention they get too much to want to be free of it.

I was in his hospital in Boston, Mass., and saw a man on a stretcher fitted with wheels who nearly knocked me over as he whizzed along a corridor, a big smile on his face. Only four weeks before he had been admitted paralysed with pain. Gerry was extremely handsome, with dark curly hair and a lovely disposition. I saw him checking in at his London hotel and be propositioned by an air hostess who was also checking in!

Gerry not only took on Elizabeth. He married her. Avril and I were invited to their wedding in Boston USA. I couldn't accept because I was in one of my poor periods. Sometimes I was rich and sometimes I was poor. Rich is better.

By this time I was getting the feel of the sentiments Mr Milligan was writing about. I wondered aloud whether I could try it. "Of course" said Mr Milligan, "who would you like to write to?"

I had only one person in mind, Lana Turner, the original "Sweater Girl" with MGM. She was a good bit older than me, at 23, and Dad described her as "Tasty"

Mr Milligan let me choose paper and an envelope. I knew that she had married Artie Shaw in 1939 and had been divorced the same year. She married Joseph Crane in 1942, and that lasted only until 1943. So she was alone and hurting, and I thought would welcome a letter. I chose an off-white paper with shiny bits in it and a dark blue ink. I still have the fountain pen I used to write to her. I've had two new reservoirs and three new gold nibs, but I use it still. I told her she was my favourite and that I really hoped she would meet "Mr Right" soon. (she met seven all told) I may have intimated that I had started the South Wales Chapter of her fan club. I addressed it to:

Lana Turner

Hollywood

America

I stuck on a stamp and put it in the post and awaited a reply. Sure enough, a month later I received a glamorous signed photograph of her.

I treasured that picture until you all moved house to Llanharry while I was at university, and the picture went missing. I suspected for a long time that our Joe had taken it.

The Bus Ticket

I was born at 40 Southall Street Brynna, a terraced house, three up three down. Downstairs there was the back kitchen, where we lived and cooked and ate and washed and ironed, a middle room, rarely used, and a parlour at the front of the house, just for show. Upstairs were three double bedrooms. No bathroom, no boiler, no stove. There was one cold water tap, outside the house, one outside toilet at the bottom of the garden, electric light (shilling in the meter) downstairs but no power points and no lighting upstairs except candles. We bathed in a tin bath in the kitchen on Friday nights.

We had lodgers. Toastie Davies and his wife Elsie and little boy Rex had the parlour and one bedroom. Mam and Dad had a bedroom and Marg, Joe and I had the third bedroom.

Dad worked at Llanharan Colliery and had to bath every day in the tin bath in the kitchen, the water boiled in a kettle on the fire. Toastie Davies worked at Werntarw colliery, the most dangerous coal mine I ever knew. I don't know where Toastie bathed. Perhaps in a bowl in the parlour. I was not four years old (Rex 3, Joe 2) when Toastie was killed by a fall of roof at Werntarw. He was brought back to our house in his black and put in the parlour. Some women in the village came in to wash him and lay him out. I think Elsie and Rex lived in the middle room until the funeral. Soon afterwards Elsie and Rex moved to a house in Llanharan, a mile away, but we remained friends for many years.

Margaret passed the 11 Plus and went to Bridgend Grammar School for Girls. The following year I passed and went to Bridgend Grammar School for Boys. We travelled to Bridgend by Western Welsh bus. All the bus number plates began with KG. Denny Roberts said that was because they were all owned by King George. We each had a season ticket which was valid for the five weekdays. I was learning the violin at school. We bought the violin off my Uncle Geoff, Dad's brother. He charged us £2 for it. He was always careful with money. Much later, when he opened a sweet shop in Hastings, Avril and I and the children went to visit him and his wife Anne (who just happened to be Avril's best friend at Hastings High School for Girls). At the end of the visit Geoff said "would the children like some sweets?" They chose modestly, thank goodness, because Geoff charged us. "That will be one and sixpence" he said.

My violin lessons were on Saturday mornings. I had a "bus pass" to travel on Saturdays. One Saturday our Joe (he who must be obeyed) wanted to go into Bridgend. Joe was what was known in the vernacular of the time as a "Heller". Rex was persuaded to take him in the bus (he couldn't be trusted to go by himself). I was given the job of meeting them after practice and making sure they got on the bus home. I was 11, Rex 10 and Joe 9. The fare was sixpence return, (two and a half p in the new money) three pence single. Rex and Joe were given sixpence each for the bus fare. Rex bought a return ticket, and for some reason Joe bought a single. When I collected them for the return journey I learned that Joe had spent his return bus fare on chips.

I had no money. Nor did Rex. I offered Joe my season ticket, which he refused on the grounds that it was valid only for week days. He was picky. He also refused to use my

Saturday bus pass on the grounds that my name was on it. He would settle only for Rex's return ticket. Rex took my season ticket and I offered my bus pass to the conductor. We sat apart, and we would have got away with it but an Inspector got on the bus . Joe was OK. He had a proper return ticket. Both Rex and I were exposed as criminals. Being a Grammar School boy I tried to negotiate. I had a legal bus pass. That was a bad move. I had given my season ticket to Rex

The Inspector was adamant. He took down our particulars and told us action would be taken.

I couldn't tell Dad. I hoped and prayed that if I did nothing it would go away. A few anxious weeks later a letter from the bus company, addressed to Dad, dropped on our doorstep.

Dad was furious. "Why didn't I tell him at the time?" "What did I think I was up to?" I mumbled and fumbled and said I was sorry. There was nothing for it but for Dad to go to Bridgend post-haste to see the Inspector.

He was working afternoons and had to be back to get down the pit by 2.30. He wasn't best pleased. He jumped on his bike and pedalled furiously (in more ways than one). It was six miles to Bridgend and six miles back. I'll never forget the words he used when he got back. "Every time my feet came round on those pedals I imagined I was kicking your backside"

I don't know what he said to the Inspector or how much he had to pay, but I wasn't taken to court and I wasn't sent to jail. That came later.

The Leap of Faith

We all carry superstitions, but sportsmen more than most. Bounce the tennis ball 42 times before serving, put on the left boot before the right and so on. My own is that I wear my lucky socks for all my bowling competition games unwashed all season long. It works for me. I rarely lose a match, and when I do lose one it's because of an aberration.

Logically, we know that the superstition itself doesn't work. But it does make us feel invincible, which is a much better attitude to have than than being diffident. And the opponent senses that you feel invincible and feels a lesser man because of it. That's how it works.

Footballers are more superstitious than most and that applied in spades to Brynna United AFC. Every Brynna boy's ambition was to get into that team. Nothing else mattered. I had just a few games in 1947/48 when Brynna was in the Welsh League Div 2. My first game, played in Brynna, was against the German POW camp which was in Bridgend. Even two years after the war the POWs, who included Field Marshall Von Rundstet, had not been repatriated. My abiding memory of that game was being taken out by a huge disgruntled German fullback who knocked me over the railings alongside the pitch. I was 15 years old, and slight. Liberal application of the magic sponge brought me round. In those days of comprehensive tackling and no substitutions the medical opinion was that if you could stand you were fit to play. I could stand so I played on.

The POWs won the game, and one of them sneered at the end " we have beaten you at your own national game".

My uncle Will, who had skulked along the length of North Africa and right through Italy during the war, said "We've beaten you twice at your national game"

My next big moment was a prize game, a visit to Penarth and its splendid ground Jenner Park. Recently demoted from Div 1, this was a professional stadium. The coach called in at Llanharry to pick up Dick Roberts and Ernie Saunders. Ernie had played for Accrington Stanley. Brynna was doing well enough financially to give "money in the boot" as expenses. I was getting £1.50 playing football at a time when I was getting less than £2 a week working down the pit.

Ernie had a mate with him, Ian Caruthers, who had played for Bristol Rovers - as a goalkeeper! He had his boots with him, and the committee dropped me, a 15 year old flying wing, to put in this has-been. Although Brynna won the South Wales and Mon Amateur cup in 1948 we were demoted into the Bridgend and District League. I never did get another chance to play at Jenner Park.

The point of this story is that Brynna won the cup because of a superstition. There were two factions in the team. One put their shorts on left leg first, one right leg first. It was causing dissent in the ranks. The committee decided that we should all jump into our shorts with both feet at the same time. This required an inelegant system. One player kneeled on the ground holding open the shorts. The other player stood in front, put his hands on the shoulders of the kneeling player, and jumped into,the shorts. You had to choose your partner carefully. Those were the days when men didn't wear underpants beneath their shorts.

Although we won the cup, the Leap of Faith WAS unpopular, and the system was dropped. So were we, out of the League. However it was revived in 1954/5 when I was playing regularly at centre-half. I invented the sweeper centre-half system, and we won the Bridgend and District Open Cup in 1955.

So it went on, in and out, success and failure. In 1976 a young chap came from St. Asaph for a Easter holiday with his uncle and aunt in Brynna. His uncle talked him up and he was given a few games. He was brilliant. He scored five goals in three games as a 15 year old. Brynna was using the Leap of Faith at the time, and young Ian Rush, for it was he, was enthralled by it. He kept it up all his life. It worked for him.

He was still using it when he joined Liverpool FC in 1980 and, using the Leap of Faith, scored a club record of 346 goals for Liverpool. He tried to persuade the whole team to use it. He was a living example of its success. In 1983/4 he bothered manager Joe Fagan so much that Fagan said " if you score a hat-trick on Saturday against Stoke we'll adopt it." Rush scored five that day and Liverpool went on to be a power in the land, and to win the Championship in 1990.

Ian rush retired in 1996, four years after the Premier League was founded. When he retired they dropped the Leap of Faith and Liverpool struggled. Couldn't get any luck.

On May 25 2005 Liverpool were playing in the final of the European Cup in Istanbul. At half time Liverpool were 3-0 down to Milan.

At half time Stephen Gerrard asked everyone except the players to leave the dressing room, including manager Rafael Benitez. Gerrard said, "In desperate times we have to use desperate measures. You remember Rushie and his Leap of Faith? Are you up for it? Are you up for it" he roared. Every player shouted "yes" and they all took off their shorts and did the Leap of Faith. Gerrard himself scored a belter in the 54th minute, Smicer scored two minutes later and Alonso four minutes after that. At 60 minutes it was 3-3 and the shell-shocked Italians lost 3-2 on penalties.

That's not the end of the story. Ian Rush split with his wife Tracy after 25 years of marriage and took up with a black-haired Irish singer/model half his age named Carol Anthony. Now Carol was friendly with the daughter of Jurgen Klopp, the Liverpool manager. She and Klippity (for that was her name) discussed 58 year old Ian's virility. Carol told Klippity that Ian still jumped two footed into his underpants every morning. "It works for him" Carol giggled, winking furiously. Carol explained that Ian had done this for every game he played in, and it brought him luck.

Klippity reported the story to her father, Jurgen Klopp. At that time, 2019, Liverpool were desperately chasing Manchester City for the Premier League title. Klopp re-introduced the Leap of Faith, and although Liverpool didn't lose another match, neither did Manchester City, and City took the title.

In the next season, this one (2019/20) Liverpool did the Leap of Faith from the start of the season and romped away to the Premier League title. Not many people know the secret of their success, but if you watch when Liverpool celebrates their title on the open topped bus through the streets of the city, I'll bet you see at least some of the Liverpool players demonstrating the Leap of Faith.

I have a faint hope that that we might see Klippity do it as well. If so, I would be able to see whether she has a tattoo in the same place as that other German girl I had a run-in with in 1950.

The Dagger Tattoo

I worked at Llanharan colliery for a year before I went to university, and there was always a job for me there during the vacations. I was the manager's pride and joy, the first from his colliery to get a university scholarship from the NCB. And a Brynna boy at that.

But I did take some holiday. In 1950, when I was 18, I used my fortnight's holiday for something different. As a mining engineer I had a remote connection with the archaeologists at the university. They set up an August camp at Llanharry, and were happy to have volunteers to help out. The dig was near the old iron ore mine, and as a budding mining engineer I was able to offer an opinion about how the people of 2000 years ago were able to discover and access the hematite to make iron. I also found a footprint in the limestone. It looked to me like the footprint of a modern tortoise, but they got quite excited about it. Said it was a new species, 57 million years old. They named it after me, Cheirothererium Hiettica.

We were in tents, and spent our days, with our little trowels and toothbrushes, discovering minute traces from which proper archaeologists could build a picture of what life was like for people a thousand or ten thousand years ago.

In the evenings we amused ourselves by telling stories around the camp fire. I told them the story about the "lunatic under the bed". It's a well -known tale, but I'll tell it briefly here. As always I like to personalise my stories to make them sound more authentic. So I said it was about my sister Margaret.

She was a newly qualified teacher at her first post in an infant school in Tring, in Bedfordshire (where the bicycle bell was invented) She had a small flat and a small dog to keep her company. The dog slept under her bed, and at night, if she was frightened, she would lower her hand to the floor and the dog would lick it. She found that comforting.

One night, lying in bed, she heard a drip, drip, drip from the bathroom. She worried about that and put her hand down, felt a rough tongue licking her hand. In the morning she rose and went into the bathroom to find the body of her dog, drained of blood, hanging above the bath.

There was a German girl in the camp. She was no more an archaeologist than I was. She was into tattoos. But she wore an academic gown at the dig for show. She came to see me the next day to say how sorry she was to hear of my poor sister's misfortune. I laughed. I told her the story wasn't true. She was furious. "You lied to me" she shouted. She had tiny fists and beat them against my chest. I apologised and said " it was just a story. That's what I do. I tell stories"

She wouldn't be placated. She drew away from me and then - I don't know if it was a threat or a promise - she undid the top button of her trousers and lowered the top far enough for me to see her latest tattoo. It was a dagger, the top of the handle at her belly button, the blade going down much deeper. I gazed at this depiction and became enamoured of her.

I'll draw a veil over what happened next. Let us say it left me feeling discomforted. But I didn't forget. When I got back to university I had a word with my friend Ron Sumption, pronounced "sumshun". Ron used to joke that 'the p is silent as in bath.' Sumption was a good looking bloke, very much like van Johnson, the American actor. He was a natty dresser all his life. He was also captain of the miners' rugby team, a position for which he was qualified by virtue of the facts that he had a little French, could ride quite well and knew his wines. He was a personable young chap unhindered by a scintilla of self doubt.

We hatched a plan to play a trick on the German girl - Sumption called her Helga the Hun. We knew where she lived in Cardiff. She lived in a flat owned by Fred Stitfall the former Cardiff City full back, in Splott. Sumption and I were in digs in Fred's own house.

The plan was that Sumption would take out Helga for a few drinks while I prepared her flat. I knew how to pick the lock. It was taught to us as part of our course. I won't bore you with the reason. I urged Sumption to keep her out until 11:30, and send her home tired and emotional. I would do the "lunatic under the bed" act which had angered her so much at the dig.

On the night in question Sumption asked if he could borrow my mac. It wasn't raining, but my mac was very swish. I had bought it in a second hand shop. It was long, Italian, very stylish. When Sumption put it on he looked the part, suave and sophisticated and comfortably rich. Off he went to pick up Helga, off I went to pick her lock.

She had a big fish tank in the flat, and I decided to take one of the large Coy Carp to hang in her bathroom. Not much blood in a carp, so I went to plan B. I went out and bought a rabbit. They have quite a lot of blood. I hung it over the bath, behind the shower curtain, and from the bedroom I could hear a very satisfactory drip, drip, drip. I put the dead carp in my jacket pocket and waited for Sumption to bring Helga home.

When I heard them at the door I slid under the bed.

They seemed to be taking a long time to say goodnight, but eventually Helga came in and flung herself onto the bed. She could hear the drip, drip, drip from the bathroom but was too tired to investigate. (Well done Sumption!). I waited. Then I realised the futility of the whole operation. Helga wasn't going to put her hand down to be licked. Helga didn't have a dog. Neither Sumption or I had picked up on this.

There was nothing for it but to wait until she was asleep and sneak out. I slid out from under the bed, went into the bathroom to collect the rabbit, and headed for the door.

Helga woke and started screaming. I went out of the door and raced down the street. It was two o'clock in the morning. I saw a hurdle on the pavement in front of me and unthinkingly leapt over it - and into a deep hole in the pavement.

I lay there winded and for an instant I thought that if I died there, in 1,000 years time some archaeologists would find the bones of a young white male with a fish in the remains of his jacket and a pile of rabbit bones in his hand. No doubt they would be able to work out how that came about.

The Pink Toenail

It was a good year to start university, 1949. The war had been over for four years, but we were a long way from normal peacetime. The coal mines had been nationalised, most of the Bevin Boys escaped, young men were being demobilised from the forces and starting at university. The more adventurous were drawn towards mining engineering.

At that time there were 15 universities and only five per cent of people went to university. I was the first from my family to go. The mining students were a macho lot. No civilising influence of women in the Department of Mining. Everyone, staff, student and lab technicians, were men. The only woman was Miss East, Prof Sinclair's secretary, and she rarely ventured out of her office.

In my group was Hevin Looker, who had fought at Arnhem, Keith George who had been in the Merchant Navy and was torpedoed a couple of times on the North Atlantic convoys, J H Jones was a professional footballer, Arthur Ball was a professional boxer, Jack Lewis was an experienced colliery surveyor. Even I, at 17, had been a year down the pit. My university fees were paid by the NCB, the local authority paid me £135 a year as a grant, I had a job to go to on every vacation and I was earning £1.50 a game at football. Dai Rowlands was the only schoolboy in our year. All the rest were experienced men of the world.

Sweets were still rationed and there were spivs selling on the black market. Cardiff Bay, now a sophisticated Mecca for the big spenders was still Tiger Bay, full of Lascars, spivs and ladies of the night. It was a no-go area for students - except for us miners, who saw it as a challenge and a bit of excitement.

I recall being separated from my fellow adventurers in Tiger Bay, teasing a couple of spivs who were trying to sell me razor blades. The blades were double sided, individually wrapped in grease proof paper. I obliged them to unwrap them one after the other because I didn't want to buy fakes. (I didn't want to buy at all. I was 17, what did I want with razor blades?). The spivs got a bit bullish with me, waving the razor blades under my nose, until Keith George rolled into view, mac hanging open, big, bald-headed, pugnacious, calling out "what the f...'s going on here."

There were some unusual antique shops and pawn shops in Tiger Bay, where I liked to wander, looking at objects brought back from abroad and foreign family heirlooms. It was in one of these shops that I found the foot. It was obviously a woman's foot. It was beautiful, perfect. It was a left foot, and it caught my attention because the middle toe had a toenail of a luminescent pink colour. You will know that on my own right foot I have a middle toe with a nail of the same colour. The Lascar who owned the shop said it was the foot of an Egyptian princess, and it was 3,000 years old. I didn't believe that, but something tugged at my heart to make me buy it. It cost me £5, which was a lot of money for me. My weekly dinner bed and breakfast cost was only £2.50. I thought I could use it as a paperweight on my desk.

Then I thought of a trick I could play on Spike Probert, my surveying lecturer. Spike had written a book on surveying but had failed to interest a publisher. His method of teaching was to read out a chapter of his book every lesson, which we faithfully copied down in longhand. He never ad-libbed. If we had a question he would tell us that either he had told us in a previous lecture, or would cover it in a future lecture. I thought I might be able to brighten up a lesson.

My plan was to get into his lecture early, sit in the front row and take off my shoes and socks. I would draw up my left leg into my trouser, and put the Egyptian foot on the floor in front of me, with the ankle poking up into my trouser leg. My right foot would be alongside it. So Spike would see two bare feet, a small left foot and a bigger right foot, both with a pink middle toenail.

I went to the Bluebell that evening for a few Black & Tans with Sumption, and we discussed the plot. We agreed what his part would be in the unfolding drama.

Sometimes life plays tricks with a trickster. I was lying in bed that night when I heard a tap, tap, tap noise. I opened my eyes to see a young girl hopping across my room. She was olive skinned with beautiful cheekbones, a fine long dress and luxuriant hair. She had a jade coloured necklace across her breast which gleamed in the light from the street lamp coming through my window. She spoke in Coptic, which is close to Welsh, so I was able to understand her. "Please give me back my foot" she said, "I've been so miserable without it. I can't get to the souk to buy the things young girls want. Please help me."

Now I'm a sucker for a sob story, and I could never resist a cry from the heart. I thought of all she had suffered for 3,000 years, and the comparatively small amount of pleasure I would get from it. "I knew when I bought it that you would come for it" I said, "I bought it to give it back to you."

She gave a cry of delight, grabbed the foot from my desk and fitted it on. She gave a little dance around the room. She was so happy I felt it was all worth while.

She said, "you've been so kind to me. I'd like to give you my necklace in exchange". She took the jade necklace from her neck and put it on my desk. Then she had another idea. "I'm sure my father the pharaoh would like to thank you. Will you come with me.?" "Gladly" I said, and she took my hand and we whirled away. I was quite giddy by the time we landed, in a great stone hall. At the other end of the hall sat seven pharaohs. The middle one spoke to me, again in Coptic, to thank me for my kindness and to ask if he could reward me in any way. By now I was drunk with excitement. "I've given your daughter her foot" I said, "why don't you give me her hand?"

He was furious. How could his daughter, a princess of an ancient Royal house, marry a coal miner? He flew (literally) across the room and shook my shoulder.

I heard Sumption's voice, "Come on, wake up, you'll be late for Spike's lecture." I stumbled awake, dressed and went to my desk to pick up the foot.

It wasn't there. But in it's place was a jade necklace. It was lying on my notes about astronomical surveying. They were sketches of the sun and the stars, all millions of miles away. It seemed appropriate that the necklace should lie there.

After I graduated I joined the NCB Directed Practical Training scheme, and as part of this I was sent to have a look at some French coal mines near Lens. I thought it fitting to take the necklace with me, and present it to the museum in Lens. I expect you can find it there today. It has a notice under it.

"Presented in memory of Captain Thomas Evans and the Countess Avdotya Alexsandrovna."

The Lost City of Cwmciwc

You will forgive me if I introduce this story with a little bit of geology. The South Wales coal seams were laid down horizontally hundreds of millions of years ago, before there were any creatures on land or fish in the sea. There were tiny sea creatures called trilobites, and lots of vegetation on land which later became coal. Silt was laid over the top of the coal seams and earth movement over millions of years caused the coal seams and the Carboniferous limestone rocks which were below, above and between the seams to buckle. As a consequence the South Wales coalfield became shaped like an elongated saucer, the longest axis being East-West. So the seams were inclined, and almost outcropped on the South side of the saucer.

In much more recent times, in geological terms, came the retreat of the glaziers at the end of the last Ice Age 10,000 years ago. The retreating glaciers gouged huge valleys out of the ground on their way to the sea. The Vale of Glamorgan was one such gouging, and the reason why you can find polished pebbles on the ground so far inland. It cut through the lip of the saucer and exposed the coal seams. Little wonder then that there were old collieries in the Brynna area.

When I was a boy there were two deep mines, Llanharan and Werntarw collieries and two closed collieries, Brynna Wood and Cwmciwc.

If you walked up Southall Street, passed Annie the Rent's, there on the right hand side was the site of Brynna Wood colliery. I never saw any sign of a colliery having been there. No spoil heaps, no old iron. It was just pleasant countryside.

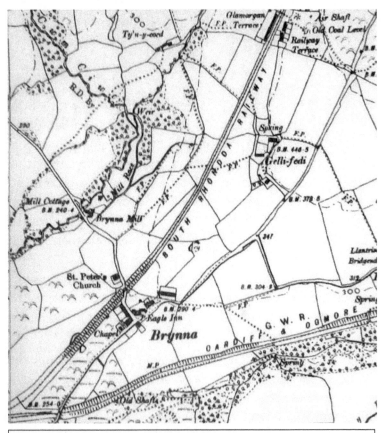

Map of Brynna showing the Eagle Hotel, the Church, the Mill and Cwm Ciwc (Welsh for Valley of the Ciwc) both North of the church.

But I'm pretty sure a colliery had been there because Mam said that her father had worked there.

Cwmciwc colliery was in the other direction. Go down passed the church and the Mill towards Werntarw. Cwmciwc was a large ruined area on the right, and to my mind didn't look like a disused colliery either. More than that, no-one knew anyone who had worked there.

It was covered with brambles, and we picked blackberries

there. Mam said that when she was a girl she used to pick blackberries there by the clothes basket, and sell them to the jam factory in Pontyclun. So even when she was a child there was no colliery there. Not only were there no signs of a colliery, but there WERE signs like those of the lost cities of the Incas and Aztecs in the forests of South America. Jumbled stones, as if a giant's hand had spread destruction all around. So I questioned whether there had ever been a colliery at Cwnciwc.

The old hermit, Guto Cwmciwc, who lived amongst these scattered stones, used to come and talk to me while I picked, but only when I picked alone. He was a kindly old man, and very wise. I had the impression that he had always been an old man.

He had a wonderful knowledge of physics, the prince of sciences, around which all the other sciences , chemistry, mathematics, geology, botany etc., knelt. It was Guto who introduced me to what is now called quantum mechanics. It got me into trouble with my physics teacher in school , who still clung to old fashioned ideas about the structure of the atom.

He also knew his astronomy. He told me about our sun being a star, and that the millions of stars we could see were also suns with their own planets He introduced me to the astonishing distances. Our sun was 90 million miles away. He said the furthest planet of our sun, Pluto, was 40 times as far from the sun, and the the asteroids, furthest away from the sun in our solar system was 2500 times as far! He said that the nearest star to us in our galaxy was so far away that if I could drive the fastest car in the world towards that nearest star it would take me 100,000 years to get there. I don't know if he knew then what we know now, that there were not millions of stars in our galaxy but billions, and that there were billions of galaxies all as big or bigger. Maybe he knew but didn't want to strain my credulity.

It was Guto's teaching that allowed me to grasp astronomical surveying when I went to university. Astronomical surveying is easy to do but very difficult to understand why it works. I understood it straight away, and taught Sumption and the others, using an orange and a golf ball.

He had a very logical way of thinking. He told me once "if you have a complicated problem, don't look for a complicated answer. Look for the simple answer. It will probably be the right one".

He told me local history in such detail that it blew my mind. He said that after the Romans left Britain it fell into lawlessness. It was survival of the fittest.

By the fifth century the fittest were well established. Local lords, and even King Arthur, who was around at the time, felt safe enough to build castles in the verdant valleys, instead of hill top forts more easily defended.

Such a castle was built at Cwmciwc. It wasn't quite a city, but it was a substantial settlement, with a lord's home and traders and craftsmen living around it. His territory stretched over the whole of the Vale of Glamorgan.

Lord Cwmciwc was a warrior first and foremost. He liked nothing better than to saddle up and go and look for a fight. The Vale was bountiful, good farming land, and under his protection his subjects prospered.

He was utterly fearless, and took his four strong sons and 10,000 men across the Narrow Sea to Lesser Britain. At that time the whole of the British Isles and a large part of what is now France spoke Welsh. He was away from home for seven years, and returned with just seven men.

His wife was no longer there. His sons were buried in Lesser Britain. His seven faithful men asked him "what shall we do, Lord?"

He said, "I thank whatever Lord is looking after me for my indomitable spirit. I release you from any obligation to me. Go forth and prosper. Share my lands between you. Take wives. Care for your children. As for me, I will remain here at Cwmciwc and watch over it".

"And did he? Did he stay and watch over it?" I asked.

The old man smiled.

"That's for you to decide, my boy" he said.

The Farmer and the Draper

The Bowen family had farmed there, on the edge of the Brynna on the way to Mountain Hare, for generations. Now there were just the three siblings, Eric, Anne and Rosie. They were all unmarried, and content to be in that state. They kept pigs, cows, geese and chickens. Rosie, approaching 50, was a bit unsteady on her legs, and they decided to get a young girl in to help out.

If there was an empire in the Brynna at that time, it was of the Dendles. The Dendles operated from a block right opposite the Eagle Hotel. They had a draper's shop and attached to it was a general store, a hardware and a seed and corn store. In later years, when I was a boy, only the draper's, run by Miss Dendle, was left. The rest had been taken over by Aaron David, with a sweet and cigarette store and, horror of horrors, a billiard saloon, where I started on the road to iniquity. I was on my way to becoming a legend in my own mind, the Joe Davis of the Brynna. And then I was banned, dashing once again my "hero" aspirations.

The Dendles had quite a large family, more than was needed to run their empire, and they gladly hired out 15 year old Mollie to the Bowens. Mollie was plain but wholesome, a good worker, who settled very well into the Bowen home. She worked on the farm as well as in the house. She cleaned and cooked and cared for the kitchen garden. As a draper's daughter she was a good seamstress and mended all their clothes very neatly. She lived in as one of the family. The Bowens paid her a weekly wage, which she gave to her mother. Her mother bought her clothes for her. As time went by she became more and more embedded in the Bowen family. She even learned to play their old organ by ear, and was able to entertain them in the evenings. The only trouble was that the only music she heard was at chapel; the only tunes she could play were hymns.

First Rosie died, then Anne, and Mollie and Mr Bowen remained to look after the farm. About 25 years after Mollie had gone to the Bowens they got a message from Mollie's mother. All her daughters (except one) had married and had left home. Her two sons had been lured away by the high life of Pencoed and moved there to live; Mollie would have to come back to the shop in the Brynna.

Mollie couldn't believe it. She had lived at the farm longer than she had in the Brynna. She knew every pig in the yard. She had seen every chicken hatch. She wandered around the parlour, touching the furniture she had polished so lovingly. She looked at all the implements in her kitchen. She could not bear the thought of leaving it all. She was 40 years of age and well settled. She had to think of a plan. She was slow but she was determined. She decided that the only solution was for her to persuade the confirmed old bachelor Mr Bowen, to marry her.

She decided to wait for the best opportunity to open the matter to him, and that would be after he had enjoyed his favourite evening meal. At the end of the meal, as he relaxed with his trusty old pipe, she said "Mr Bowen, you know that my mother has said that I must go back to live with her".

" I don't know about that Mollie, you'd be better off here."

"I can tell you, Mr Bowen, that I don't want to leave the farm. I've grown accustomed to it, but we need to find a way for my mother to agree."

"Well, I can't think about that now, Mollie. I'm off to my

bed, so I'll say goodnight."

"Goodnight Mr Bowen" said Mollie. He went to his room at the front of the house, she to her's at the back of the house.

The next day Mollie tried again. "Will you go and talk to my mother, Mr Bowen?" He did that willingly, but he wasn't very persuasive, and didn't get the right answer.

She nagged at him gently. "Who will cook your meals when I'm gone, Mr Bowen? Who will look after your clothes? Who will look after the farm when you go to market? Who will tend our kitchen garden?"

He sucked at his pipe, miserably. "I don't know, Mollie. I don't see any solution. I'm going to bed now. Goodnight Mollie."

The next day, after supper, she said, "Mr Bowen, have you ever thought of getting married?"

"Getting married? I'm 60 years old. What girl would want to marry me?"

"You don't have to marry a young girl, Mr Bowen, You could marry somebody of 40, say, my own age. That would work out".

Mr Bowen went to the mirror hanging in the hall, which he used to put his hat straight. He saw a grizzled old face, roughly shaven, missing teeth, not at all attractive to the gentler sex. He didn't want to take a chance of asking and being refused.

"From what I've heard, Mollie, wives can be a nuisance, always wanting to spend money in the shops, not getting their work done as they should, always needing something new."

"It doesn't need to be like that Mr Bowen. If you married

me, for example, things would stay exactly the same as they are now, except that you wouldn't have to pay me any wages. And I wouldn't need any new clothes, because Miss Anne and Miss Rosie's clothes are still in their wardrobes. There's years of wear in them yet."

"Oh, I don't know about that Mollie. That needs a lot of thinking about. I'm going to my bed now. Goodnight Mollie."

The next day he said to her, "Did you really mean what you said yesterday about you marrying me? Everything would stay the same as it is now but I wouldn't have to pay you any wages?" Mollie agreed that she did mean that, and Mr Bowen went to see her mother and father. They were quite pleased to think that their daughter was to marry a well-off farmer, and agreed at once.

The wedding day was set. Mrs Dendle, ever romantic, had wanted the wedding to be in the tiny medieval mother church up the mountain, only 25 yards by two yards in size where we went once a year for a service. The vicar said it was no longer consecrated. So the wedding took place at St. Peter's church, and the wedding party retired to the Dendle's house for some sweet sherry and a few dainty sandwiches. There was a cheering crowd of drinkers outside the Eagle, offering advice to Mr Bowen, which he didn't seem to understand, and eventually the newlyweds went back to the farmhouse.

"Well, that was quite an exciting day for me" said Mr Bowen, I'm quite worn out. I think I'll go off to my bed. Goodnight Mollie."

"Goodnight Mr Bowen" said Mollie, and went off to her own room.

The Day my Heart Broke

As soon as I grew out of the *Dandy*, the *Beano*, even the *Hotspur*, I developed an overwhelming interest in heroes. They didn't have to be good heroes, as long as they were utterly fearless. I was 12 years old.

I read avidly of the heroes of Ancient Greece, of Hector and Hercules. I delved into the stories of Alexander the Great, and Kubla Khan. I even begged my mother to let me have a Cossack breakfast - a raw onion and half a pint of vodka. I devoured stories of the Mabinogian, the fifth century warriors of Wales, whose only desire was to fight to the death. Taliesin was one such hero, and Peter named one of his sons after him.

Not for me the woolly history taught in my Grammar School. They gave me 1714 to 1914 as my period to study. How could 1714 - 1914 be of interest to such as me? I ranged the mountain, standing (fairly) tall in the bitter winds, the dust and the flies, staring with steely blue eyes across landscapes seen aeons ago by heroes of the past. What is life without risk? What was there a schoolboy could do to join the pantheon of the bravest of the brave?

I discovered the brave words of Theodore Roosevelt, and have kept them close to me to this day. It goes:

> " it is not the critic that counts, nor the man who points out how the strong man stumbled, or where the doer of deeds could have done them better. The credit belongs to the man who is actually in the arena, whose face is marred by

Brynna Infant School and the author as a schoolboy

dust and sweat and blood; who strives valiantly; who errs and comes short - again and again; who knows the great enthusiasms; the great devotions, and spends himself in a worthy cause. Who, at the best, knows in the end the triumph of high achievement. And who, at the worst, if he fails, at least fails while daring greatly, so that his place shall never be with those cold and timid souls who know neither victory or defeat."

I knew I would have to wait some time to become a hero of any consequence, so I determined to adopt a hero in the interim, and learn from him. I cast about, but the Brynna was not a fruitful place to find heroes of consequence. Arthur Ware had come home on leave wounded, but he had been shot in the bum, obviously running away, so no sort of hero. I was beginning to despair.

And then I found him. In Llanharan. Jack Kennedy was a middle aged man, a veteran of the First World War. He had a little business delivering bread and delicious cakes around the Vale of Glamorgan. I can still see his Iced Slices, his Chelsea Buns and his fairy cakes. The smell in his van was delightful. All that summer holiday I helped him. I travelled round the Vale with him, running to his favourite customers with their favourite cakes. I would gladly have helped him for nothing, but at the end of the day he would give me a few of any cakes left over.

He wasn't very tall, but he had a noble bearing, a soldier still. He had a scar across his face. I had no doubt he had other wounds across his chest -never his back- bayonet wounds, bullet wounds, shrapnel wounds. He never spoke of them. I never asked.

He had a dignified charm, and I copied what he did.

I copied his walk, I copied the way he tied his shoelaces. I copied his forbearance in the face of acute pain.

I expect he had medals, but he was too modest to display them. I didn't know what rank he had held in the army, but I imagined that he had been a young officer, sent raw to the trenches of the Western Front and behaving nobly, giving his last cigarette to a dying Tommy. I was on the point of forming a fan club. I didn't want to share him, but I believed he deserved a wider recognition, maybe even a statue. It could go up in Pontypridd Market, Mecca of the Rhondda shopper. I imagined the ladies passing by and rubbing his blessed toecap for luck.

Then that day arrived. We were in Coychurch, a pretty little village about five miles from the Brynna. Mr Kennedy was talking to a woman at the door of the White Hart, and she asked him the question. How did he get his scar? Was it in France?

I was standing close, bathed in his reflected glory. I was about to share THE STORY NO-ONE KNEW.

He said:

"No, I had flat feet. I spent the whole of my war up to my knees in blood and bullets in Newport Barracks. How did I get this scar? I had a bit too much to drink one night and fell through a pub window"

The Cloak

The two modern bungalows opposite Brynna School were destroyed by a German bomber, fleeing for home across the darkened countryside. It is thought that the bomb aimer saw a glow from a nearby train when the fireman opened the firebox to shovel in coal. The bungalows were flattened but no-one was hurt.

The bungalows housed two families, the Collins and the Matthews. Brian and Edie Matthews were very friendly with David and Joan Collins. In fact, you could say that they lived in each other's pockets. Not only that, but their grown up children were friends. Edie's daughter and Joan's son were courting.

Before the war the two families were quite prosperous. They dressed well and could afford little luxuries ; the families enjoyed going out together.

Joan was quite slim, almost severe in her dress, She had been brought up in a Puritan family in Llanharry, that den of iniquity. She had bettered herself by marriage. She wore little make-up and never went to the hairdresser's. Her hair was long and straight and wound on top of her head. It had streaks of silver/grey. She always behaved properly. She was very reliable.

Edie had a fuller figure, corset bound. She took a great deal of trouble with her make-up, and was never seen without it. She was more colourful in dress without being flamboyant. She had her blonde hair permed regularly. She maintained high standards in all respects. Edie and Joan enjoyed going on shopping trips together.

Edie and Joan set off on one of their regular visits to Pontypridd Market. They started early. They took a bus to Llanharan, a bus from there to Talbot Green and yet another bus to Pontypridd. It was a long day but it was worth it. The market was huge, dozens of stalls selling everything you could think of, from material to clothes pegs, food and drink to hardware, rugs to bedding.

The market was always flooded with women from the valleys, who spoke a patois different from the sophisticates of the Brynna and the Vale of Glamorgan. They heard one valley woman, looking at curtain material, say to her friend, "pink I do like, blue I do rather. But puce, o Deuce (derivative of Duw, Welsh for God) I do go scatty for puce"

Joan and Edie moved companionably through the crowd. They each had a list of what they would like to buy, and all day to do it. Then they saw the cloak. It was on a wire frame and it was breathtaking. It was long, a dark blue, almost purple colour, with a shimmering electric blue lining. The stitching was exquisite. It had a silver inlay around the neckline. The lady assistant said " that's just arrived from Paris, but they made a mistake in pricing it. That price is below cost price. That's the only one I've got. When it's gone it's gone. It's an exact copy of the cloak worn by Catherine the Great, Empress of Russia. The original cloak is being exhibited in the Hermitage Museum in St. Petersburg". She pronounced " Hermitage" in the French way, she made a little moue with her scarlet lips.

Edie said " it is really beautiful, but I can't afford it". Joan said " were you thinking of buying it for your Emily?"

"No" said Edie, I was thinking of buying it for myself, but I really can't afford it. "I think you are very wise, dear" said Joan, "but, truth be told, those who are fortunate enough not to be skinny wouldn't look good in that cloak". "What are you suggesting, dear" said Edie, "do you think I couldn't carry it off? But in any case, it's too expensive, and that's the end of it".

"If you don't want it, Edie, I wouldn't mind buying it for myself" said Joan.

Edie was appalled. "You can't do that" she said, "I saw it first"

"But you don't want it, said Joan, "it's a bit of a dog in the manger attitude I must say"

There was a stand-off. A breathless moment. But they had been friends for such a long time that they wouldn't let a cloak come between them. But there remained an undercurrent of suspicion. The two ladies separated to go their own ways to the stalls they wanted, but discovered that by circuitous routes they had both arrived back at THAT stall. The cloak was still there.

They went away again in confusion. And then Edie saw her chance. A gang of youths from Dolau were causing trouble, knocking over boxes. Dolau youths were always doing things like that. That is why they were universally disliked. In the furore, Edie said" I'll go and find a street walker". She darted off, saw Mrs Morgan from William Street in the crowd, stuffed money into her hand and asked her to go and buy the cloak and take it home for her.

She got back to Joan, the ruckus was broken up by the street walkers, and Joan and Edie completed their shopping and made their weary way home. But it was Joan who went, secretly and alone, to Pontypridd the following day.

Life continued much as before for the two families, until

the day of the chapel whist drive , which in those days was a dress-up affair. Edie went into the cloakroom to deposit her new cloak. The girl taking the coats said, "I see you've been to Pontypridd Market, Mrs Matthews."

"Why do you say that?" asked Edie.

"Well, that's the sixth cloak like that I've checked this evening, including your neighbour, Mrs Collins."

The Mushroom Field

It's a funny thing, picking mushrooms. It doesn't matter how large or small your family, or how many of them like mushrooms, you have to pick every one in the field. You can't leave any for the next picker. It's different scrumping apples. You tend to leave a few for the man who owns the apple tree.

So it was when I went up past St.Mary's Hill to my favourite mushroom field. All over the field I spotted those white caps in profusion. And off I set to gather up every last one of them.

I had just about finished picking the mushrooms when I spotted a host of rabbits feeding at the far end of the field, on a little hill sloping down to a stream. I also spotted a ferret or a weasel dragging away one of the rabbits, much bigger than itself. It held it in a vice like grip on the back of the neck. "Hello" I thought, " I'll have that for myself and take it home for dinner". So I took it from the weasel. The rabbit was still alive, so I held it up by the ears to give it the karate chop I had seen in the films.

Then I heard the sweetest music coming from nearby. If you are looking for magic, you could do worse than be a young man in a green, green mushroom field, with rabbits nibbling close by, on a warm September day and listen to Heavenly music by the side of a stream. I dropped the rabbit and it scampered away to join its fellows on the hill. I followed the sound of music to a little arbour at the edge of a wood. A woman sat on a bough by the stream, playing a stringed instrument on her lap. Later, I learned it was a lute. I was entranced by the music, and by the woman. She was the most beautiful woman I had ever seen. She saw me standing there.

"Hello" she said, "are you a musician?"

"Yes I am" I said hurriedly. I was but a second violin in the school orchestra. I wasn't a very good violinist, but I wanted her to feel an affinity towards me.

"Will you sing for me?" I asked boldly.

Her head was bowed, but she looked up at me without lifting her chin. Her eyes were enormous, and I was lost in them. I have endured many winters and I know now that this look is an art form perfected by women, but at that time I was just a youngster on the brink of manhood.

She played a love song, a song of unrequited love. All Welsh love songs are of unrequited love. I don't know how the Nation sustains itself. I waited for the end of the song.

You know that light travels at 196,000 miles per second, but when you snuff a candle the light flees away much more slowly than that. You can see it fade. It is the same with sound, although sound travels much more slowly than light. At the end of a song the last note slips into the first moment of silence. For me, the first moments of silence are part of the song. I hate it when audiences start to clap before a song ends, robbing me of that breathless moment. She, too, felt that first moment of silence, another affinity between us.

"Where do you live?" I asked.

She waved a long chiffon clad arm over her head and behind her.

"I saw you save that rabbit's life," she said. I didn't disabuse her. "You are a kind hearted young man. You call back to me the days of my youth, when I was so happy. I was taught music at the conservatoire in Jakarta. I was really beautiful in those days . I performed in great houses and on the concert stage. I was pursued by handsome young men. And then..........."

She stopped. Her feet were bare and she wriggled her toes. I didn't want to disturb her melancholy. I took off my own shoes and socks, and was immediately sorry. I have always had neat feet. Some people have said that my feet are my best feature. But compared to hers, naked alongside mine, they looked clumsy. Quickly I plunged my feet into the stream. She smiled at me, and slid her feet into the stream, close to mine, as quietly as her last notes had slid into that moment of silence. Her feet and ankles were golden, the skin almost translucent. I could see the fine bones beneath the skin.

"What happened next?" I breathed.

She sighed. It was like the sound of silk tearing, like a woman saying "yes." I waited for her to go on. "Life happened," she said, "that's what happened. I grew older. My looks faded. I had less attention paid to me. My mother died." She paused again, and I thought that was the end. Then she said:

"I got married. I married a man who thinks more of money than of love. Unlike you, he has no interest in music. He leaves me alone too much. He spends a lot of time away on business. He's away now. He won't be back for a week or more."

Her speaking voice was as enchanting as her singing voice. I let it caress me as I watched the water in the brook caress our bare feet. There was some significance there, I thought, some affinity.

I was spiralling into uncharted territory. I didn't know what to do. So I went back to basics. I recalled Dad's three rules for a happy life. "You won't go far wrong," he said, when we were having that Dad/son talk when I reached a certain age, " you won't go far wrong if you follow these three rules

> 1 never play cards with anybody called Doc;
>
> 2 never eat in a cafe with "Ma's" or "Mother's" in the name, like "Ma's pantry " or "Mother's Kitchen" for example.
>
> 3 never get tied up with a woman who has more problems than you"

Well, it was obvious to me that this woman had a lot more problems than I did, that's for sure, and, tempting though it was, I made my excuses and left, as they used to say in the News of the World.

It wasn't quite as brutal as that. Against my better judgement and against my basest instincts, I gave her half my mushrooms before I left. I could still hear her music, calling me like a siren, until I reached the Llanharan road.

When I got home my mother said to me, " where are your socks?" "They fell off" I said, "they fell off when I was picking mushrooms"

The Imaginary Friend

Not many people know that our Jeanette didn't talk until she was four years old, and even then she talked with a lisp. When she started school her first teacher was our Margaret, who was doing her Teacher Training practical at Brynna School. There was a boy of Mordicai who teased Jeanette about her lisp. Margaret called him out in front of the class and told him off severely.

When Margaret finished her practice Jeanette got herself an imaginary friend as her champion. He was the same age as me. He had been in my form at school. Islwyn lived in a farm near Heolycyw, and she would threaten anybody who bullied her with setting Islwyn on them.

Jeanette talked about him freely in the house, and we all went along with it. We began to learn a lot about him. He wasn't very big but he was very strong, living on a farm. He lost a bit of one finger in some farm machinery which caused him to miss the 11 Plus.

Even now, seventy years later, Jeanette still talks about him. He still lives on the farm, but now he manages it alone. Even at his great age he still climbs up ladders onto the roof of his house. He still sees Jeanette in chapel, and he always talks to her about me. "Remind me to your John," he says, "We were in the same form at Brynna School."

But it was in those early years in Brynna, when he became a young man, that he earned a reputation that he didn't deserve.

It really started with Annie Owen the Rent. She was

bothering Mam to go and do a bit of cleaning for her. Mam already had her hands full, a house to keep, seven children to take care of and a husband who came home from the colliery every day in his black. In addition she was cleaning the brass in the chapel.

Annie Owen the Rent was a very difficult woman to refuse. Dad said, "Tell her a little white lie. Say our Wendy has a cold or something." Mam, being big in chapel, didn't want to do that, but thought it the lesser of two evils.

The crunch came when Annie Owen the Rent came down when all the kids, in obvious rude health, were out in the street playing. "Can you come up now?" Annie Owen the Rent said to Mam.

In desperation Mam said, "I can't come now. I'm waiting for a man to come and ease that bedroom sash window." Strictly speaking, it was Annie Owen's house, and she should have been easing the window, but she saw a chance to save some money. "What's his name?" she asked. "Islwyn," said Mam, in a panic. "I could do with a handyman," said Annie Owen, "Can you ask him to come to me?"

Annie Owen the Rent was quite shrewd She thought that if a poorish person like Mam could afford him he didn't charge very much for his work. And since rich people always paid less to workmen than poor people did, Islwyn would cost her, Annie, even less. In the end, Mam had to ask Mr Tebby, next door, to ease the window, and she gave him one of her blackberry tarts for his trouble.

A couple of weeks later Annie Owen the Rent was complaining that Islwyn had not turned up, and wanted to know where he lived, so that she could go and see him. Mam didn't know where he lived, she could only leave a message for him. "He's a scoundrel," said Annie Owen, "I think I saw him skulking by the allotments the other day. He's got shifty eyes."

Later, when somebody had stolen some cabbages from her garden, Annie Owen said, "it must have been that wretch Islwyn".

But nobody could catch him. No-Good Boyo said he'd caught a glimpse of him, couldn't recall his face, but said he was wearing an army blouson. Mr McAndrew said, "Islwyn? Yes, I think I know him. He did a couple of jobs for me not long ago. He's not much good, but he's very strong".

So the image of Islwyn grew. We began to know more and more about him. Then there was a really sad event. A simple girl in William Street was led astray and wouldn't say who was responsible. She cried a lot, but Annie Owen the Rent had no doubt who the father was. "It's that rogue Islwyn. Somebody told me he has flat ears, and that's always a sure sign of depravity." She shouted at the poor girl. "It's Islwyn, isn't it? Don't deny it!" The poor girl wept but didn't say yes or no. " I knew it!" said Annie Owen.

There was a hue and cry, many people thought they saw him, and his description became more and more acute. Red hair, thin arms, always wearing that army blouson.

Through all of this Jeanette remained faithful. She insisted that her hero, Islwyn, would never behave like that, and she thought that Annie Owen the Rent was a vicious old bat. The only hope seemed to be to find the real perpetrator or perpetrators.

Islwyn was seen by different people in different places - Pencoed, Pontyclun, Brynteg, even at a football match, and sometimes at the same time. He could be in two places at once! He was the Scarlet Pimpernel of the Brynna. "They seek him here, they seek him there..." Everybody thought he was having a laugh on them.

Then one day Mam was in the back kitchen having a cup of tea with Auntie Rose, when there was a knock on the front door. Mam was pouring tea, so Auntie Rose went to answer it. Rose came back, "There's a man at the door wants to talk to you"

"What does he look like?" said Mam

"He's not very tall, with red hair and he's wearing an army blouson"

"Did he give a name?"

"Yes, he said he's called Islwyn. He wants to say goodbye to you, and to pass on a message to Jeanette, because he's got himself a 1939 Standard Flying 12 and he's just leaving to go to Scotland."

"Tell him to come in," said Mam, "He can have a cup of tea and and a few Welsh Cakes to see him on his way"

But when Rose went to the door he had already gone. Mam was in two minds. She was sorry he had been driven away, but she drew comfort from the thought that perhaps she hadn't told a lie to Annie Owen the Rent about the window easing.

The Assassin

They arrived in Llanharan by train, then by bus to the Brynna. The evacuees. Forlorn. That's what they looked like when they were unloaded on the pavement opposite our house. There were about a dozen of them, wearing coats, gas masks and a label tied to their coats bearing their particulars. They didn't have much luggage, considering they were here for the duration. They were all of primary school age, between about six and ten. With the benefit of hindsight I can see that they were lost frightened little kids, bewildered, tired, sent to a strange land, a mining village, with people speaking very fast in an accent they couldn't understand. They just wanted to go back home. To us, at the time, they were just curiosities, out of place in the Brynna.

There was no preplanning. No prior arrangements for taking them in. People just turned up to choose a child or two, like picking a football team on the school playground. The village bobby was on hand to make sure no disreputable person took on a child, and a woman in charge wrote down the new addresses of the children.

Mr Thomas in William Street worked for the Water Board and had a car. He was also a good snooker player. After the war I saw him play an exhibition match in Llanharan against Joe Davis, the world champion snooker player. So Mrs Thomas had the first choice of evacuees. They already had two boys of their own, Clayton, my age, and Aneurin, our Joe's age. She wanted two girls. I thought that if she had wanted girls so badly we could have given her a couple of ours, Anne and Margaret for example. But we missed our chance.

She chose Sheila Hinch, a very pretty girl who looked like Shirley Temple, and Marie, who was a bit taller, had an olive skin and was nicely dressed. Mrs Thomas was obviously delighted at the prospect of buying clothes for the girls. The dear things had brought their clothing coupons as well as their ration books.

We couldn't take any evacuees, as our house was already full, but soon all the evacuees were allocated , and all found places at Brynna School.

One of the boys, Fatty Driver, was the butt of our jokes. He was so fat he couldn't run very fast. He had no chance of catching us when we teased him. He used to be in tears of frustration. We thought it a huge joke, but Mam thought we were being cruel. She commanded me to invite him to tea in our house, and laid on a scrumptious spread. The allotment provided fresh lettuce and cucumber with plenty of salt for sandwiches, radish and spring onions, ditto, shop cakes and Welsh cakes, tart and jelly. When Mam called us to say tea was ready we all rushed to the feeding frenzy. Fatty Driver wasn't used to that speed. Our Anne was already at the table in her high chair, her sharp little elbows clearing space for herself. She could put it away even then. She had a full round tummy that glistened like butter.

We had a policy of eating everything that was put on the table. Not a crumb was left, because we knew that if we left one piece of bread and butter Mam would cut one piece less next time. But even we had a job to clear the table on that occasion.

Mam found out that Fatty's name was Vincent, and he and his mother lived alone in London. Mam felt sorry for him. "Don't you worry, Vincent," she said, "our John will take care of you". I wasn't very pleased. It was bad enough having to lug around our Joe, without adding another nuisance to my burden.

I earned a few Brownie points with Sheila Hinch, though. She said that it was very good of me to have invited Fatty Driver to tea. I shamelessly took the credit for that. She was a VERY pretty girl.

But it turned out that Fatty wasn't such a bad chap at all. As my "friend" he was safe from teasing by the other boys, and I taught him some country crafts. I taught him how to make a wooden whistle. You need a good penknife and some care. You cut a switch of Hazel, fresh, this year's growth, of about a finger length and half an inch thick. Cut a V notch half an inch from one end, the first cut vertical, and half way through the stick, the second at 45 degrees. Then you wet it - saliva is good for that - and tap the bark all around with the handle of the penknife. After a while the bark separates from the wood inside, and you can pull off the bark sleeve. All that remains is to cut a bit of wood off from the V notch at the shortest end, so that your breath can reach the notch, gouge a groove down the middle of the stick from the notch to the far end, and slide the bark collar back onto the wood. Hey Presto, it's a whistle. Only a one note whistle, but good enough to referee a football match with.

It was while we were setting night lines in the river to catch a few trout that he talked to me about his life in London. It was quite tragic, really. His father had been killed at Dunkirk, but before he'd left for France with the BEF he had called together Fatty and his younger brother (who subsequently died young) and brought out the service revolver of his own father from the First World War. He told them not to tell their mother, and keep the revolver hidden.

If the Germans invaded , it was every man for himself, and if they were going to die they should take one or two Germans with them.

Fatty's mother found it difficult to manage on just a soldier's pension, and had to take in a lodger. He wasn't a nice man. He was a spiv, treated Fatty's mother with disdain, and behaved as if he owned the house. The boys hated him, but Fatty's mother needed the money.

One weekend she had to go and visit her sick mother in New Malden, and planned to stay there one night, a Sunday night.

The lodger has taken over the boys' bedroom on the first floor, and the boys had to sleep in a poky little attic. They reached it by a fire escape ladder which came down to a balcony outside the two bedrooms on the first floor.

On the Sunday night when the mother was in New Malden the lodger came home drunk again and went to bed. There was an air raid on. The boys didn't go to the air raid shelter. Fatty's little brother took the revolver and climbed down the ladder to outside the lodger's room, and into the room. He was snoring like a pig, and sweating. Fatty's brother put the revolver to the lodger's ear and pulled the trigger. He climbed back up the ladder and hid the gun under his mattress. Amid all the noise of the air raid no-one heard the gun shot.

The next day, Monday, the two boys went to school, and when their mother came home she found the lodger in bed with a hole in his head. The Police were called, but there were no clues. The Police suspected that some other gang of spivs had killed him for their own reasons, and he wasn't missed very much anyway.

A bit later I was talking to Sheila Hinch again. By now I

was creeping up the list of her admirers. I was probably in her top three. I asked her, casually, "did you know Fatty Driver's younger brother in London?" She looked puzzled. "I know the family. He never had a brother, older or younger. He's an only child."

It was then that the true story hit me like a bolt from the blue. It wasn't Fatty's brother who had shot the lodger. Fatty himself was the assassin. I can tell you that from then on I was a lot more careful not to annoy him.

The Taming of the Shrews

Robert Finch, known to his friends as Dick, was a good looking young man. He was also a very good tradesman, a cabinet maker. He lived in that house at the end of Church Street with a Monkey Puzzle tree in the front garden. It overshadowed the house, but he couldn't cut it down because it was the only Monkey Puzzle tree in the Brynna.

He built a workshop in his back garden, fitted out with a workbench with a vice, a lathe, a wood stove, using his off cuts for fuel, clamps and glue kettle for boiling glue, various planes and his tools neatly arranged on the walls. His workshop was his palace. He ate his meals in his house.

Few people in the Brynna could afford to buy his work. His furniture was beautiful because he took so much care with it. He took so much care with it because he loved wood. He loved wood like a mother loves a new-born baby. He loved to look at it; he loved to smell it; he loved to caress it. When he put his hand on teak he could feel the softness of the oil buried deep within it.

He made pieces of furniture which were snapped up by Howells of Cardiff, who sold them on. Finch furniture could be found in elegant drawing rooms across Wales, from Aberystwyth to Abergavenny.

He did some jobs for local rich people, one of whom was Lady Blandy Jenkins, who lived in Lanelay Hall in Llanharan. I met Lady Blandy Jenkins only once, when I was a small boy. I had won a race for small boys on Llanharan Sports Day, and she presented me with the prize of two Bob (10p in the new money), my first professional earnings.

She lived in this grand house with her daughter Amelia. Amelia had a good social life. She rode with the Llangeinor Hunt, she belonged to the Young Farmers' Club and the Young Conservatives. She was like Princess Anne. She had impeccable manners but no-one ever got close to her. She was reputed to be arrogant and imperious and "didn't suffer fools gladly". No man had ever come near to winning her heart. Few would have risked incurring her displeasure.

Robert Finch was called to Lanelay Hall to deal with a great table in the dining room. He spent a week just preparing the table, and had just finished doing that when Amelia came swinging in through the French windows. She was wearing a dress with short floaty sleeves. Her sun-kissed arms glowed. Robert was stroking the table, lost in the beauty of the wood. Amelia said "that looks really beautiful". He smiled. "Lady Blandy Jenkins wants me to French Polish it". "Oh no, you mustn't" she said, "it would be a shame to cover up that gorgeous wood". "I believe you are right" said Robert, "just feel that wood, rub your fingers along it. The wood is alive. It's like touching a human being"

The golden hairs on her arms seemed to shiver of their own accord. Robert ran his fingers up her arm, against the lie of the hairs. His hand was rough but gentle on her arm. The next thing Amelia knew was that she had her arms around his neck. She was besotted. She was his, gladly and unreservedly.

They were married in a grand ceremony in Cardiff. The Marquis of Bute, a former lover of Lady Blandy Jenkins (and putative father of our Granny Evans' niece, her sister's daughter) gave away the bride and they held the reception at the new Cardiff Airfield. Amelia piloted her two-seater plane down to St. Tropez for the honeymoon, and then moved happily to the house in Church Street to begin married life in the Brynna. They were a devoted couple.

Not so devoted were Mr and Mrs Tebby, who lived next door to us in Southall Street. They were like Howard and Pearl in Last of the Summer Wine. Mrs Tebby had a cat she called Toby. Mr Tebby called him "666" because the cat attacked him with tooth and claw for no reason whatsoever. When Mr Tebby complained to Mrs Tebby about it she said that he must have done something to upset it, and scolded him. Mrs Tebby didn't like Mr Tebby very much, and the cat liked him even less.

Mr Tebby was also a carpenter. He had a workshop a little further up our back lane. He was pleased when he heard that Robert was planning to marry another virago. He couldn't wait for them to come back from honeymoon to tease Robert about it.

"How are things?" He asked Robert.

"Everything in the garden is lovely"

"I hear your Amelia has a bit of a temper"

Robert was annoyed that anyone should criticise his blushing bride. "Not a bit of it.".Everyone in the village knew about poor old Mr Tebby's marriage predicament. "I put that right from the very first day"

Mr Tebby was intrigued. "How did you manage that?"

"As soon as we got home I kicked her cat so hard that I killed it. I know that sounds harsh, but I had to establish who was master in the house, and it worked." Robert, of course, had done nothing of the kind. In fact, Amelia had had a cat. It died of natural causes, and Robert made it a beautiful rose-wood coffin and buried it with a ball of Angora wool for company at Lanelay Hall. Amelia thought that was very sweet of him.

The story gave Mr Tebby cause for thought. He thought of his own miserable existence, and he determined to do something about it at last.

He walked down from his workshop full of resolve, and came into his house through the back gate, into the kitchen. Mrs Tebby was sitting in the armchair, knees slightly apart, ready to spring up if he trailed any dirt into her house. The cat Toby was glaring balefully at him from across the room. Mr Tebby was dreaming of at last becoming master in his own house.

He squared his shoulders, ignored his wife, marched purposefully across the room and aimed a kick at the cat. It wasn't a very accurate kick. It barely grazed the cat. The cat sprang spitting into the air. Mrs Tebby fetched him a blow across his ear which knocked him sideways.

"You ungrateful scoundrel!" she said, "What has that poor animal ever done to you to deserve such treatment? It's shown you nothing but love and affection and you reward it with a kicking. I ought to give you a good kicking."

Mr Tebby, lying on the floor, wailed, "Too late, too late"

He was remembering the little ditty which his mother (who came from Cardiganshire) used to sing to him when he was a boy:

"Never trust a bird with feathers at his throat,

Never trust a weasel who pretends that he's a stoat,

But the most important rule, if you want to stay ahead

Give her cat a kicking on the day that you are wed."

A Bit of a Do

Dad was on the Parish Council in Brynna for a short while. He was wise and well read, but a reluctant Parish Councillor. He had a lot on without that, working hard six days a week down the pit, mending the shoes of so many children and looking after a 30 rod allotment.

There were two high spots in his career as a councillor. One was a trip to Cardiff by the whole Parish Council to inspect some new-fangled fluorescent street lighting - a trip which came to nothing. The second was even more exciting, an invitation to a smart dinner party.

Lady Blandy Jenkin's daughter Amelia, who lived in the Brynna with her husband Robert Finch, had produced twin boys, and Lady Blandy Jenkins decided to mark the occasion by inviting all the VIPs of the Brynna to a dinner at her home, Lanelay Hall in Llanharan. The VIPs included the whole of the Parish Council, with their wives, Mr Davies, the Superintendent of the chapel, the new vicar of St.Peter's church, (the new vicar is always the new vicar until he leaves, when he becomes the old vicar), Mr McAndrew, who was a Public Speaker, Mr Thomas the Water Board, both of the teachers at Brynna Primary School and Annie Owen the Rent.

Mam and Dad were a bit nervous about it, but it was like a Royal Command, so a good deal of thought went into what to wear. Dad had a good three piece suit, but Mam had to have a new dress. She went to Cardiff to buy it, no expense spared.

The author's parents on a chapel outing to Barry Island.

Mr Thomas had a four seater car, and he kindly offered Mam and Dad a lift. That was a great relief. They didn't want to take a bus to Llanharan and then walk the half mile or so to Lanelay Hall - and especially not to take that route on the way back home. Mr Thomas wore what his wife, who was Dorset born, called a "Ronald Coleman mistarsh," so, perched in the driving seat, he looked like a professional chauffeur.

They drove up to Lanelay Hall with great aplomb, and went in through the front door. A servant curtsied and took their coats and led them into a reception room where they were offered a choice of sweet sherry, or red or white wine. Dad wasn't very good with strong drink, so he knew he would have to take it easy. Mam was also unused to strong drink, but had an amazing capacity for it.

Mr and Mrs McAndrew came in. Mr McAndrew put back his left leg to make a bow to Lady Blandy Jenkins and trod on the tail of a large Labrador, which leapt in the air and knocked Dad over. He crashed into a table holding glasses and drink. Lady Blandy Jenkins was very gracious, begging his pardon for the dog's behaviour and making sure he was alright. She ordered some servants to clear up the mess and insisted on personally taking Mam and Dad into the dining room and to their seats. Dad wasn't hurt. He was a very strong man. Lady Blandy Jenkins was very solicitous.

There was a very long menu, with French dishes as well as English. There was more cutlery for each person than most people had in their own homes for the whole family, but they managed to steer their way through it. There was watercress soup to start, then a small fish dish, and then a sorbet, to clear the palate. This was followed by a choice of chicken, cooked the French way or roast beef, with fresh vegetables. There was a lovely creamy pudding and cheeses and fruits to follow.

The waiters were dressed in their finery, and other waiters brought around wine throughout the meal. They addressed the guests as "Sir" and "Madam" - "more wine Madam?". There were speeches. A brigadier in full dress uniform and medals proposed the Loyal Toast, and they all responded "God save the King". Someone else proposed a toast to "the coal industry and all the brave men who worked in it, and long may it continue". That, too, was rapturously received.

Then the twins were brought in, in the arms of nursemaids, to great acclaim and lots of "oohs" and "aahs" from the ladies. Robert Finch, the proud father, proposed a toast to the boys, named Robert and Richard, and wished them a long and happy life. Lady Blandy Jenkins replied to the toast on the babies' behalf.

She said how propitious it was that the twins had been born on the second Sunday after the Lord's Test, and she believed that Richard was showing signs of being a left-hander. She was a keen follower of the noble game. Her late husband had scored a century for the army against the MCC.

She kept a cricket pitch in the grounds of Lanelay Hall. Many years later, when I was about 21, I had the privilege of playing on that ground. I was in the Llanharan Colliery Officials team in a knock-out competition. I was keeping wicket. At a critical point in a closely fought final the batsman, playing forward, missed the ball. I caught it and took off the bails. I didn't appeal. He was in his ground. The square leg umpire asked me, "Did you appeal?"

I said, "No, I didn't."

He said, "I think you should."

I said, " How Zatt?"

He said, "Out!"

We won the game. I have the trophy still. But it's not a trophy to me, more like a badge of shame.

Then Lady Blandy Jenkins whispered something to one of the servants, who returned with dishes containing something they didn't recognise. "I expect they've saved the best until the last," said Mr McAndrew knowingly. The dishes contained what looked like thick black stubby pencils. Perhaps a German delicacy. Mr McAndrew was the bravest. He picked one up and put it into his mouth, chewing away. Two or three other men followed his example. It was obviously hard work, and, by the look on their faces, not very tasty. However, good manners required that they continued chewing and swallowing.

The brigadier was looking on in some amazement, and after he thought it had gone on long enough he took one from the dish, snipped the end off with a little gadget he took from his waistcoat pocket and set a match to the other end. Cigars have become popular since, but at that time nobody in the Brynna, not even Mr Thomas the Water Board had seen one.

From then on it went downhill a bit. The cigar eaters, on top of rich food and lots of wine, felt decidedly queasy, and the new vicar volunteered to walk them home to the Brynna a little over a mile away. They were all sick on the drive, one of them over the vicar's brand new boots, permeating the lace holes. The boots never lost the smell and the vicar, Christian though he was, never forgave the poor man.

Dad came out of it rather well. Not only was he a hit with Lady Blandy Jenkins for his stoicism, he more than held his own in a conversation with the brigadier, who discovered that he had served in the same regiment as Dad's father on the Western Front in the First World War. "Salt of the earth," the brigadier declared his Sappers to be, and he shook Dad's hand warmly. There was a hint of a tear in the old soldier's eye.

Robert Finch was also impressed by Dad, and made

him a lovely wooden cigarette case with his initials L.G.H engraved on the lid, which Dad cherished. I think I saw the cigarette box on Mollie's mantlepiece in Tenby when I visited a couple of years ago. It was full of thimbles.

The Arbiter

I started school before the old king died. I know it was before the old king died because I remember that all us school children were taken out of school to stand alongside the railway and wave as the train passed carrying the king and Queen Mary. I didn't see them on the train. One boy boasted that he had seen them and they were wearing red, white and blue.

I made friends with Tim on my first day at school. He was much smaller than the rest of us and he had a crippled leg. He lived on a farm with his father and younger brother George. We all got a third of a pint of milk a day at school, but Tim, because he was so small, got a spoonful of malt as well.

He liked to be with us bigger stronger, faster boys. He got a vicarious pleasure from it. He enjoyed our company and our antics. He was never bullied. He had calm grey eyes, like a wolf. If he was ever threatened he just looked at the bully, and his gaze said, " Yes, I know you are bigger than me, but when I'm older I will remember you, and I'll make you suffer". Tim and I were inseparable.

We both sailed through the 11 Plus. I came sixth in Glamorgan, Tim came second. We both went to Bridgend Grammar School, both of us in the express stream, four years to the School Certificate instead of the usual five. He enjoyed my triumphs on the running track. He was so pleased for me when I started playing football for Brynna , at 15. He used to help the team by selling "pullers" on match days. He would accompany me and Alan Reed to dances at Tonyrefail. We had to walk there and back. It was about six miles each way, and must have been hard for him with his bad leg, but he was so grateful for letting him come with us. He never got a girl, but enjoyed watching us trying.

He became the wise man of our bunch. He was the Arbiter. If we had a spat he would call us together, point out that we had more in common than in opposition and make us friends again. Whenever there was a dispute he would be called in to resolve it. Once, we had decided to teach a teacher in school a lesson. We were discussing damaging his car, or peeing in his wellies. But Tim talked to us about balancing risk and reward. On a 50:50 chance, like tossing a coin, you don't risk £1 to win £1. In the case of the teacher, there was a reasonable chance of being found out and being expelled. And for what? There are more ways than one to skin a cat. We boys were all natural risk takers. What is life without risk was our motto. But Tim's erudite reasoning prevailed.

By the time we got to sixth form we both chose to study English, History, Economics and German. We sixth formers sat in the front benches in assembly. One day the Headmaster, addressing the whole school about behaviour, illustrated it by saying "fools like young Hiett (he meant my brother Joe) bringing a dagger to school and saying it was for sharpening pencils". I was seriously embarrassed and wanted to kill him. Tim talked me out of it.

I was destined for the Civil Service, when I was old enough to sit the entrance exam. Tim for greater things. I recognised even then that I was in the presence of a great diplomat of the future, and I looked forward to a distinguished career for him, even a knighthood, and my position as his special friend.

After my first year in the sixth form I decided I didn't want to moulder in an office. I went over to Llanharan colliery to talk to the manager. He told me about the National Coal Board's university scholarship scheme to produce colliery managers. It seemed ideal to me, that I could do some hard manual work until I was too old for that (about 25) and could then be a colliery manager. So I left school and worked down the pit for a year before going to Cardiff University to study mining engineering. Tim completed his Higher School Certificate and won a scholarship to Oxford where he studied PPE. The scholarship was worth only about £70 but the prestige was great. Scholars wore short gowns, other students wore long gowns. Scholars were allowed to walk on the grass in the quad, others were forbidden to do so.

We started university at the same time. We both became involved in our new circumstances, and we drifted apart a bit. Then our family moved from Brynna to Llanharry, and I had no call, on my short visits home, to go to the Brynna. I heard that Tim had dropped out after a year at university and gone back to the farm. After I graduated I was moved about a lot to various collieries. Then I got a job as colliery under manager in Somerset. I got married and started a family and moved back to Wales to work. I was working very hard and didn't find time to seek out old friends. Then pits were closing all around me and I applied for a job at Coal Board HQ in London, and was offered the job.

Before I moved to England I made an effort and went to the Brynna to see Tim at his farm. It was a raw March evening. He was sitting in his parlour with his books. His housekeeper and his farm boy were in the kitchen. He was pleased beyond belief to see me. He looked very tired. He had been ploughing all day. He was wearing moleskin trousers and a plaid shirt. His hands and his hair were clean. He was the same age as me, but already an old man. His small body was more twisted, and when he got up to fetch some bottles of cider (our favourite teenage drink) he walked slowly, and his limp was more pronounced. I wished I had visited him earlier. But we were at ease from the start, as if we had never been parted. He didn't have television, just a wireless and his books. He had always been an avid reader.

He had a noble head, and one of those voices which always had a chuckle in it. It was so sad. Here was one of the finest minds in the kingdom mouldering away on a tuppenny-halfpenny farm. If only. If only he'd finished his degree. He would have been a power in the land by now.

I talked to him about Avril and Peter and Sian. I told him about my new job in London. I told him, jokingly, "I've been down the pit all my life. I don't know what a filing cabinet or a woman looks like. I know they're both five feet tall and grey in colour, and that's about it".

He said, "John, you are a highly qualified and very experienced mining engineer. You will be a breath of fresh air in Hobart House. You will be one of the very few mining engineers in that office. You were down the pit only last week. Every one of those people enjoying the good life in that office are doing so because of you and your colleagues, who have slaved away underground. Go up there and show them what's what. It's time you enjoyed the fruits of your labour." He was so pleased for me. I think I made him happy.

I asked him, "how about you Tim? How are you doing?"

He said " I need to tell you from the start; people thought I left Oxford because I flunked it. You know me well enough to know that I wouldn't do that. I was enjoying the university experience very much. I sat at the feet of J R Tolkein and C S Lewis. They were two of my tutors. As a scholar I had rooms in the college itself. I shared my staircase with the ghosts of great scholars of the past. It was inspirational."

Outside the window the light was failing. It seemed like an epigram of his life. An owl was awake. He lit an oil lamp.

"Then I went to the doctor's, and he told me that I had Crohn's disease, and had only five or six years to live. At the same time my father died."

I called out in distress.

"I'm still here John, fifteen years later. But now it's near the end. Don't fret. Everything has an end, and I'm ready for it. At that time, George was just coming up for his Higher and wanted to be a vet. It's not a very good farm. It wouldn't support two people at university if I had to get in a manager to look after it. I could see no option but to leave Oxford and take care of the farm."

"I was able to send George some money now and again when he went to university. It was never enough, and he grumbled about that."

"It takes a long time to become a vet, and I can tell you that the struggle was getting harder every year. When he graduated he wanted his share of the farm to set up a practice. The whole farm wasn't worth much. Half a farm would not have kept either of us. So I took out a loan, with the farm as surety. I bought George a practice in Pencoed. He's doing very well, I'm pleased to say".

"Do you see much of him?" I asked.

He hesitated. "I saw him today. I was out ploughing. He waved to me as he passed in his car. He has a very nice Audi."

He looked down at his hands. He seemed embarrassed. "To be honest, I think he's a little bit ashamed of me, because of my infirmities. He doesn't want to introduce me to his posh friends. He knows a lot of important people, and I know he's very busy".

"I had a letter today which reminder me that the bank loan, plus interest, falls due this October. The farm will have to be sold to pay it. There won't be much left afterwards."

I was horrified. I was 35 and in my prime. I had overcome so many crises down the pit I felt I could handle any problem put before me. "That's not going to happen, Tim, " I said, "I'm going to sort it out."

He put his hand gently on my arm. "You've been a good friend to me, John, all those years. I've always been very grateful for that. We've shared a lot of good times. You can"t imagine how much pleasure it's given me to remember. Go to London. Enjoy your new life. Don't worry about me. No need. I'll be gone before October."

Mrs Floyd's Diary

It was a bit like the Old Curiosity Shop, that sweet shop at the top of Southall Street. The Floyds weren't making much money out of it. There was such a variety of sweets there; some of them had been in the shop for decades, and you got good value for your halfpenny.

Mr and Mrs Floyd came to the Brynna when they got married in 1900. They did not mix socially with the Brynna people, partly because they were from London and partly because they were Jehovah's Witnesses. They had joined as teenagers in London, when the cult was just becoming popular. The Jehovah's Witnesses seemed to them to offer a haven against the excesses and inequalities of the Victorian age. "Humanity is in a sinful state" they were told, "Come to us, follow our teachings, and be saved"

They were a nice enough couple. They behaved properly. They were clean and tidy. It didn't take them very long to abandon hopes of converting the people of the Brynna. In 1914 Mr. Floyd, although a Pacifist and a conscientious objector, joined up. He wouldn't fight, but he was prepared to serve on the Western Front as a stretcher bearer. He had passed his St. John's Ambulance Certificate as a teenager, and willingly learned more, so that he was promoted to the field hospital. He wasn't a doctor, but he was a very useful aide. After the war he came back to the Brynna and resumed his quiet life as a shop keeper. He was one of the first in the village to instal electric light upstairs. It was my friend Tim and I, a couple of years before WWII started, who spotted something odd about their life style. Their shop/home was the last house in Southall Street, before a bend in the road turned it into Top Row. Between Southall Street and Top Row was a dirt track which led to our back lane. So the Floyd's house could be approached from the front, the back, and the side. There was just the two of them in the house, and their bedroom was in the front of the house. We could tell that by the light in that bedroom at nights.

So why, Tim and I wondered, was there a light in their back bedroom every day at dusk, and a soft voice talking there? We made a point of playing marbles by their wall, near that back bedroom, so that we could listen to what was being said. It sounded like a woman talking to a child, and sometimes we heard a lullaby as well.

Once Mr Floyd came out of his front door and saw us. He challenged us. "You should find a flatter place to play marbles," he said, "It's too steep here in the lane."

"No, it's alright Mr Floyd," Tim said cheerfully, "We're playing little ring, not big ring, so the slope helps."

We had to be more careful after that, but we did once sneak through their back gate to listen under that window. It was definitely a woman's voice, and she was definitely addressing a child. I mentioned it, diffidently, to Mam, but she put it all down to my imagination. "They don't have any children," she said, "and I've never seen any child in the shop or in the garden."

Storm clouds were gathering over Europe. There were more important things to worry about than the strange behaviour of the Floyds. Soon war broke out, sweet rationing came in and we were in the sweet shop less often. Getting older, we lost a bit of interest in the Floyds, but would, just for old times' sake, sometimes stand by their wall at dusk and listen. The litany didn't change much.

We moved on. The war ended. I went off to university. Mr Floyd died in 1951, aged 71. Then on February 6 1952 three things happened. King George died, and as a consequence all enjoyment was curtailed. We even had to cancel the university Mining Society's annual dinner in the Park Hotel in Cardiff. For us this was even more momentous than the king dying. The annual dinner was the time when the VIPs of the National Coal Board were invited to see their future colliery managers behaving disgracefully in a posh hotel. It was expected of us and we didn't want to rob them of enjoying memories of their own student days, of moving pianos, drinking too much beer and singing rude songs.

The third thing that happened that day was that Mrs Floyd died, and the terrible secret was out. Because of the king's death there was no news on the wireless except commentary on his life and death, and sonorous music. Nor was there much else in the newspapers. It was only after the coroner's inquest that the secret came out, and by that time it was old news, and not widely reported. It transpired that the police had to break in after the shop remained closed for a couple of days. They found Mrs Floyd dead in her bed, and in the back bedroom they found a shrine. The remains of a nine year old girl was in the bed; there was a jar of wilted flowers on the dressing table. There were photographs of a young girl displayed around the room. The curtains were pretty, and so were the bed covers. The toys and games were neatly stacked.

There was a diary.

Mrs Floyd started writing the diary in 1900, and continued until Mr.Floyd's death in 1951. Fifty years of a dull life. It was like reading Alan Bennett. She wrote about leaving "sinful" London to find peace in a small village. She found that the Brynna was not entirely without sin, but decided to make the best of it. She became pregnant in 1901. She was too afraid of her child getting besmirched by sin to tell anyone, and Frank, her husband, delivered the baby in the house.

"She is an angel," wrote Mrs Floyd, "She is so beautiful, so precious. We've named her Angela. We have decided to protect her from the rough elements outside by keeping her indoors and not telling anyone about her. Angela is delightful, but she's not very strong."

The diary told how Angela grew up, happy and contented, with loving parents. Her home was her whole world. She didn't miss other people, other children, because she didn't know about them. She heard noises from outside the house, and her mother told her that when she was old enough and strong enough they would take her out and introduce her to it.

But she never did get old enough or strong enough. By the time she was eight years old it was evident that she was going to die soon. Angela wasn't unhappy about that. She wasn't afraid to die. She was looking forward to going to Heaven, where she would meet The Lord, and where she would welcome her parents when their time came. She chose some hymns for her funeral, and asked if they would release some coloured balloons for her. In 1911 she died.

"She's just closed her eyes," read the diary, "She is so beautiful lying there. I can't believe she died. She's just stopped breathing. I just can't bury her in the ground, looking so lovely. I'm going to keep her for a little while."

But Angela didn't decay. She continued to look as if she was simply asleep. After a few weeks Mrs Floyd wrote, "I've suddenly realised. The Good Lord has not taken Angela from us. She is just in a state of suspended animation. When

The Lord comes he will touch her and she will awake again in perfect health."

The diary recounted that she continued to visit Angela every evening at dusk, year after year. Angela continued to look beautiful. Mrs Floyd talked to her and sung to her, telling her all the news. She bought her a new dress every Easter. Mr Floyd had stopped going into the room a few months after her "death". He was almost pleased to go away to war in 1914. When he returned after the war he found that Mrs Floyd had maintained her vigil faithfully. Angela, she reported, was still beautiful, just waiting for The Lord to arrive to awaken her.

The diary continued through the interwar years, through the Second World War. The village changed, but nothing changed in the Floyd household. When Mr Floyd died in 1951 Mrs Floyd just waited to follow him, and did so in 1952. Her last entry in her diary was a quotation from Gerard Manley Hopkins "the world is charged with the wonder of God. It will flame out, like shining from shook foil."

The coroner at the inquest had read the whole diary, and was very moved by it. He said that Mrs Floyd was a good woman, a devoted mother and wife, and she was blessed that her daughter Angela's body had not deteriorated over all those years. "It was a miraculous comfort for her," he said. He asked the medical examiner, Dr Evans, if he could explain why Angela had continued to be preserved. Dr Evans said, "She didn't. We found a skeleton in the bed. It had been a skeleton for forty years."

The '47 Freeze

We woke up that morning to a new world. During the night six feet of snow had fallen. It was the Spring of 1947. In some places the drifts were ten feet thick. No-one was able to go to work. No-one could go anywhere. Our immediate thought was "every man for himself". Dad and I set about it. The girls were not much help and Joe was just being Joe. Wendy was a babe in arms and the other girls were doing housework as best they could without damaging their fingernails.

Dad and I got to the outside tap, not far from the back door, so we had water to drink. Then we had to dig our way to the lavatory at the bottom of the garden, and at the same time to the coal *cwtch* and to the shed in the garden, where Dad had stored his King Edward potatoes under ferns we had cut in the Autumn. By mid-morning we had coal, food and water and a lavatory and were able to go and help the community.

The bake house was on our back lane, only two doors from us, so we cleared that, so that Mr Davies could bake his bread; then we went to help Mrs Smith who was a widow with only girls in the house. The problem was that the snow was so thick we had nowhere to put the snow we were clearing. By the end of the first day the Brynna was still covered, but traversed by canyons of snow ten feet thick. It was beautiful but surreal.

The men couldn't go to work on the second day, either. It wasn't cold and the sun was shining, but there was thick snow everywhere. Clearing it was like a military operation.

The war time spirit returned. We still couldn't cut a cabbage. The allotments were under a thick blanket of snow, by this time with quite a crispy top. The men of the village, mostly tough strong coal miners, put their backs into it and we were all enjoying the experience. By the end of the second day the main road was clear, but there were no buses running, so we couldn't go to school.

The girls in our house (except baby Wendy) were still 'potching' about pretending to do housework, and shrieking excitedly whenever they put their noses outside the door. Margaret, at 16, was pretty sensible. She was always put in charge whenever Mam had a new baby. The other four girls had their own hierarchy. Anne, 7, thought she was in charge of that group, Mollie thought that Anne was not in charge, Jeanette just wanted to look pretty, and Wendy was a baby. We men were in our element, doing important work.

On the third day the Red Cross arrived, bless them, to see if anyone needed help. We had already got to everyone in the village and all were managing quite well, thank you very much. Then someone remembered Mr Perry.

Brynna sat at the North end of the Vale of Glamorgan. Going North from the village the ground rose steeply to the plateau, which went on to form the Brecon Beacons, a bleak place even in summer time. Mr Perry lived alone in a house right on the edge of the plateau, and about half a mile or so from the Brynna. He was a tough old bird. He worked at Werntarw colliery and, Summer and Winter, he walked down to the village, dressed in his pit clothes of vest and trousers, no coat, to catch the bus to Werntarw. The lane he walked down was lined by banks and hedges, and the snow was up to the top of the hedges. It must have been ten or twelve feet thick in some places. There was no chance of getting a vehicle up there. We reckoned the snow was just as thick up at his house. Mr Perry would be without food, water or heating. Even this tough old man, we thought, would need help.

The plan was that the Red Cross men would go up there on foot, dragging a sledge of provisions and an oil stove and paraffin. I was 15 and able as any man. I knew the mountains well. I had spent a lot of time there picking wimberries. I wasn't very heavy and was less likely to sink into the snow, so I volunteered to show the Red Cross men the way.

When we passed her house Annie Owen the Rent came out and offered to help. We thought about it. She was a big strong woman. Dad said that when he first met her he didn't know whether to shake her hand or throw a saddle over her. On the other hand, if she went through the crispy snow surface we would have a devil of a job to pull her out. So we said thank you but no thank you.

It was hard going. We couldn't clear the snow. We couldn't walk on it. We had to skate up there on our bellies, like water beetles on a pond. I consoled myself with the thought that on the way back from the top of the mountain I would be riding on the sledge at 100 mph, landing in the village to a hero's welcome, and walking into 40 Southall Street for a cup of tea and a piece of cake. Some hope. Those girls would have eaten up any remaining cake.

There weren't any landmarks to find our way, but at that height, on top of the pristine snow, I could see distant things by which I could orientate myself, such as the headgear of Llanharan colliery.

It was a wonder world. Dazzling white everywhere, beauty and danger at every step. The Red Cross men were finding it heavy going, dragging that sledge. I didn't have any part in that. My job was to be a pathfinder.

It took us half a day to get there. I have to confess that I went wrong once or twice, but I got them there. They were completely exhausted, and what we saw wasn't good news. Mr Perry's house was buried in snow up to the eaves. There was no smoke coming from the chimney. We feared the worst.

I made my way over to the house. I could just see the top of an upstairs window. I cleared the snow from it and banged the side of my fist against the window frame. "Mr Perry, Mr Perry" I shouted. There was no reply.

I turned to look at the Red Cross men. They were too tired to help. "try again", one said, in what I thought was a hopeless voice. I banged again on the window frame, harder this time. I thought I might have to break the glass and crawl in. And what would I find? It had only been a couple of days, and he WAS a tough old man.

"Mr Perry, Mr Perry" I shouted.

A querulous voice answered me, "Who is it? Wadya want?"

"Mr Perry, Mr Perry, it's the Red Cross"

He said "Bugger off! I gave last year."

The Swap Shop

It's not easy, trying to earn an honest bob as a kid in wartime, and I just hate it when someone tries to rob me. The Swap Shop took place every Saturday in the Brynna, where people would gather to swap and buy and sell. It was the E Bay of the 1940s. I had swapped a working toy car for a cine projector that wasn't working. It had no light. I had thought I could use a candle, and tried it out in the air raid shelter in Granny Evan's back garden. But of course it was hopeless. I didn't have any film anyway. So I swapped the cine projector for a wooden birdcage.

I caught a pair of nightingales and put them in the cage and took them to the swap shop. They were singing away quite happily and attracted a lot of attention. Sam Dyke from Top Row offered me £1 for the pair, which I refused. I didn't like him. He was a bully and a ruffian and thought he was a tough guy. He'd never had a job. He had a gang. He came back and offered me £2 which I refused again. "These are nightingales" I said, "not sparrows. They sing sweeter than any bird in the world". Eventually he offered me £5 which I accepted.

"Bring them up to my house" he said. So I carried the cage up to Top Row. His house had a long concrete path through a jungle of a front garden. At the door he took the cage from me and said "wait here".

I waited about 20 minutes then knocked on the door. One of his gang came to the door. "Where's Sam Dyke?" I said, "I want the £5 he owes me."

He looked at me. "Don't get above yourself" he said, "That's Sam Dyke you're talking about. He"ll eat you for breakfast".

"He owes me £5 and I won't go until I see him."

"Better come in then." He was amused at my persistence.

Sam Dyke was lying back in a beaten-up armchair. He might have been a tough guy, but he evidently wasn't a very successful one. He was wearing a Humphrey Bogart type trilby, and spoke in the vernacular of the actors in American crime films. Casablanca had been shown recently in Llanharan.

"Wadya want, kid?"

"I want my £5."

"You'll end up with a concrete overcoat," he said, mixing his metaphors, "Clear off!" He tipped the brim of his hat with his finger, then pointed the finger at me. "Here's looking at you kid". It didn't sound so menacing in a Welsh accent coming from a broken-down arm chair.

I knew that he wouldn't give me the money in front of his gang, but I also knew that I was going to get it, and that I was going to make him suffer as well. I never believed in making threats. If you make a threat you've got to be prepared to carry it out. In any case, why give advance warning and let him prepare? Just do it. I stared at him for a long moment, turned on my heel and left.

I went to talk to my friend Tim, the genius of my own group. I wanted to frighten Sam Dyke and humiliate him, and to get my £5. We talked it through.

Sam Dyke had an old aunt who lived by the Mill, and he went down there every Wednesday to see what he could scrounge. I waylaid him, dressed up as a pretty young girl.

I wore one of Margaret's skirts with white ankle socks and daps on my feet. I wore a blonde wig from Mam's dressing up box, with a headscarf. I had a young fresh face and really shapely calves. When he arrived I said, "Excuse me sir, could you help me please?" He wasn't usually in a helpful mood. His normal stance was taciturn. But he couldn't resist a pretty face. "What can I do for you Miss?" He probably thought he could take advantage of me.

There was a spring near the river bridge which gave very cold and very clear water, almost medicinal, greatly prized in the village. "I've dropped my pail just under the bridge, and I can't reach it. You've got nice long arms, could you reach it for me please?"

The stones near the bridge were quite slippery, because of the splashes from the cold spring. He had to tread carefully, hold onto the bridge with one hand while he leaned over to look under the bridge for my non-existent pail. "Can you see it sir?" I asked. He leaned a little further, and I kicked him in the back of his knee. He fell into the river with a very satisfactory splash, and I raced away up the hill. I knew he'd never catch up with me before I got rid of my disguise.

Phase one of the plan successfully completed. Sam Dyke had been dispatched by a slip of a girl.

The coup de grace took a little longer to prepare. It involved the Three Card Trick. Tim talked to one of the teachers at school who was keen on magic tricks. In turn he introduced him to a friend who was in the Magic Circle. Magic Circle members are sworn to secrecy about their tricks, but Tim was such a smooth operator, with his broken little body and high intellect, that he persuaded his new friend to reveal the Three Card Trick to him.

Tim and I rehearsed the trick until I was expert at it. I

added a trick of my own. I introduced a small hesitation at the end, so that anybody who watched carefully would find the lady every time.

I set up the table and chair in the swap shop, playing for halfpennies and pennies. Those who took me on had a one in three chance of winning anyway. We were not sure that Sam Dyke was bright enough to spot my hesitation, so Tim, after playing and winning every time, moved into the crowd and spoke to a boy from Top Row, showing off that he'd spotted my fault, the hesitation, and that he could win every time. He knew the boy would report to Sam Dyke. Tim gave me the wink when he knew that Sam Dyke had been told.

Sam came over to my table, said, "move over, Kid, let the dog see the rabbit". He actually let me win! I used the hesitation and he let me win. He wanted to disarm me before he raised the stakes. It was serious stuff now, five bob a time. His friends were egging him on. "Play it again Sam" they cried. The call spread around the Square, and Sam Dyke loved it. He loved being the centre of attention. For some in the crowd he was a local hero, like Dick Turpin. And there were some, I'm sure, waiting to see that cocky little Grammar School twit (me) get his comeuppance. Sam Dyke tested the hesitation tip he'd received. He followed it twice and won. He disregarded it twice and lost. He knew the secret. He was ready for the big time.

He said, "Do you want to raise the stakes, Kid? Just one last time?"

I said, "OK, just one last time. How much?"

He took two of those big white five pound notes out of his pocket and threw them casually on the table. The crowd fell silent. That was more than a couple of weeks' wages for a man. I couldn't scrape together more than five pounds, some of which I had won from Sam, but Tim came to my aid. He laid a five pound note on the table. His life savings, £20 in all, to the winner of the final hand.

I worked the cards, made my small hesitation, not on the Queen but on the 10 of spades. He was really up for it. He reached forward with both hands, one to pick up the rest of the money, one to flip over the card. "Here's the lady, Kid," he said, and turned over the 10 of spades.

I didn't say anything. I took two of the five pound notes and gave them to Tim. I scraped up the rest of the money and put it in my pocket. I waited until he stood up to go. I pointed my index finger at him. "Here's looking at you Kid!"

The Bonfire Man

It's a funny thing. There are some men of excellent character and behaviour who are treated less than respectfully by their fellow men. Such a man was Mr McAndrew. He was trustworthy, erudite, unfailingly courteous, caring of people in general and of his workmates in particular. He was a Public Speaker. I heard him at a public meeting talking passionately about pneumoconiosis, the coal dust disease, the scourge of coal miners, which turned fit young men into old men sitting in the corner coughing their lives away. It was because of men like Mr McAndrew, speaking out about this dreadful affliction, that the National Coal Board, much later, found the answer to the problem and spent the money needed to implement it. Yet he had no friends. He was wasted on the Brynna. A prophet has no honour in his own land. He would have done better elsewhere.

The war ended with a period of upheaval. We had a new government under Clement Attlee, the coal mines were to be nationalised, rationing remained and I was beginning to turn my attention from winning the war to consider what I would do for a job when I left school. Astonishingly, while our troops stationed abroad awaited repatriation and demobilisation, scores of refugees from all over Europe were able to pour into our country.

During the war, no new wood had been available to the public. It all went to the war effort. All old wood was salvaged and used for repairs and making new furniture. As a consequence, the famous Brynna Bonfire had been stopped for the duration. A tradition of decades stopped by Mr Hitler.

Mr McAndrew decided it was time to restart the bonfire and put it to a public meeting where it was heartily endorsed. It had never been an ORGANISED bonfire. Anybody could and did contribute to it. It was built on the old railway line down by the recreation ground, high enough for everybody to see it from the many vantage points around. Crowds used to come from far and wide to join in the fun.

From the beginning of October people began to bring anything that would burn. Bits of wood, old chairs, worn out tyres. Children collected dried cow pats from the fields, carrying them back like stacked dinner plates. They were particularly welcome as they gave a distinctive pungent odour when burnt. Clippings from apple trees gave a sweet smell and holly burned really fiercely. The pile grew to a giant size.

I could remember the bonfire from before the war, but now I was big enough to do something constructive for it. I scoured the woods, collecting old tree branches; I knocked on doors asking if they had anything they wanted burning. I wasn't the only boy doing that. All the village lads - and some of the girls - were enthusiastic about it. Uncle Bill wasn't back from the war, but Uncle Tim contributed some broken cricket bats he'd been asked to look after when the war stopped village cricket.

There was just a little cloud on the horizon. There were three very unsavoury characters skulking in the village, refugees from somewhere like Transylvania we were told. They were caught stealing bits from the bonfire. A guard had to be put over the bonfire at dusk, but these three ruffians dared to steal again, and were caught again. Mr McAndrew gave them a good talking to, but since nobody spoke their language they didn't understand. Mr McAndrew was very cross and raised his voice to them, "Do you understand?"

He reported them to the policeman who walked them to Llanharan and pointed them in the direction of Llantrisant. And good riddance to them, we thought.

Dad provided a bag of big potatoes to go in the bonfire, the butcher, bless him, produced a string of sausages, the Sisterhood made a lot of jellies. More and more goodies followed. Suddenly all was goodness and light. The war was over , the Brynna Bonfire was back on course and everything was right with the world.

The evening before bonfire day, coming back from Youth Club, I saw some movement in Mr McAndrew's back garden. It was the same three foreigners lurking there. I dared not attract their attention, and, coward that I was, I didn't tell anyone about them, because they looked so ferocious. I thought they would kill me as soon as look at me, without a second thought.

I WAS very worried. Why were they there? What were their intentions regarding Mr McAndrew? Were they seeking revenge because he put the police onto them? The next morning I heard no reports of any trouble, but when I went to the bonfire I was shocked to see a life size guy on top of the bonfire. My imagination ran riot. Had they killed this good man and put his body on the bonfire? If they had it was too late to do anything to save him. If they hadn't I'd look foolish if I brought up the subject. The men of the village were putting the finishing touches to the bonfire. Surely they would have known if anything was amiss?

We expected Mr McAndrew to come along and light the bonfire just before dusk, but he didn't turn up. I think it was Mr Thomas the Water Board that did the honours. He made a pretty little speech. (He didn't mention pneumoconiosis). He said how good it was that we were back to normal, and that the Brynna Bonfire was a testimonial to all the suffering and hardship of our brave boys - and civilians - over the past five years.

We had a band! Girls from the school under the guidance of Miss Bull. She is so old that not only did she teach me, she also taught our Mam. Some girls played the comb-and-paper, others played the Kazoo. Mollie played the Kazoo she had bought at the swap shop. Anne played the comb-and-paper because she spent all her pocket money on jewellery. There was a little boy with a drum who banged it out of time with the band. Everybody sang along with them, *Roll out the Barrel, Tipperary, We'll Meet Again* and *Auld Lang's Syne*. There were tears in the eyes of music lovers.

It was a tremendous bonfire. It was too hot for anyone to get anywhere near it. They had to light smaller satellite fires to cook the potatoes and sausages. At the end the centre of the bonfire collapsed with a roar. I watched the guy fall into the inferno. It was like an explosion. Everybody cheered except me.

A good time was had by all, and we all went home tired but happy. It was my first grown-up Brynna Bonfire.

Mr McAndrew didn't turn up at all that evening and I again had that guilty feeling. I dreaded what might have happened to him because of my shortcomings. I didn't see him around the village. My guilty conscience prevented me from asking questions.

When Christmas approached I could hold back no longer. I said to our Margaret, who was a friend of the McAndrew girl, "I haven't seen Mr McAndrew now for a while. Is he alright?"

"Why" she said, "didn't you know? He was appointed Miners' Agent in the Durham coalfield a couple of months ago. I think he's coming back here for Christmas and then the whole family's moving up there. He's done very well for himself."

Colliery winding engine headgear. In 1913 there were 620 coal mines in South Wales alone. Now there are none.

A Year in the Life of.....

Bang! bang! bang. It's so noisy, a mine shaft. It's 700 yards deep, and two cages, attached to guide ropes, whiz up and down the shaft at some speed. The steel ropes attached to the top of the cages go over the headgear wheels and onto a huge drum in the winding engine house. The drum revolves, one cage goes up, one down, passing each other in the middle of the shaft. At the bottom the pit bottom men push the full tram into the cage, knocking out the empty. At the top the banksman pushes the full tram out and an empty one in. Bang! Bang! Away go the cages, winding coal.

The shaft is a bottleneck, the only way to get coal out of the pit. Which is why the manager wants to have as much time as possible to wind coal. All the men have to be down the pit by 7 o'clock, which means that some have to start going down at 6.30. The miner's day starts even earlier than that.

I was barely 16 on my first day down the pit. Stumbling out of bed at crack of dawn; downstairs Dad had already lit the fire, had the kettle on for tea and the frying pan on for the full English. Get dressed in my pit clothes, walk with Dad and a crowd of other men and boys across Brynna Wood to Llanharan Colliery, about a mile away. It was a big pit, 1000 men, raising 1000 tons of coal a day.

I had been to see the manager, Mr Hughes, whilst still at school, and he had promised me he'd get me a Coal Board scholarship to go to university when I was seventeen to learn to be a colliery manager. As soon as the summer term ended I started a sixteen week training programme, on the surface, consisting almost entirely of shovelling stone from A to B in the morning and shovelling it from B to A in the afternoon. Now I was ready for my first day of real work.

I was caught up in the excitement, milling around with men waiting to go into the cage. Last cigarette before stepping in. While men were underground there was no craving for a cigarette, but as soon as their heads popped out of the blackness into the blessed sunlight at the end of the shift they were gasping for a fag!

When men are wound, the cage is not quite as fast as when winding coal, but it is still scary/ exciting, as are all first impressions underground. Steel ropes whipping as they haul trains (called journeys) of iron trams with iron wheels on iron rail tracks of two feet gauge. The half hour walk into the coal face, cap lamps piercing the pitch black, passing journeys of full and empty trams, and belt conveyors. Men carrying their tommy boxes, some carrying tins of explosives, some carrying flame lamps for gas testing, shotfirers wearing on their belts a leather wallet with detonators, and carrying their exploder. How warm it was at that depth!

Arthur Scargill said that underground, with its noise and its dust and its danger was like Hell. "It has everything that Hell has, except the fire" he said. I didn't see it like that. It was a man's world. I loved it from the start. Yes, it was dangerous; at that time 500 men a year were being killed underground. We had one fatality in my first year. A young shotfirer fired a shot, went back in to take a look, a fall of roof killed him. He lived with his young wife in a bungalow on the road to Pencoed. He was about 25.

I was put with an old man digging a steep roadway. He'd got a shotfirer to fire a few holes, and I was the one shovelling the debris into a tram while he watched. All for

39/6d (nearly £2) a week. He was getting £5 15s. On my first day the manager passed by, saw me sweating snobs and fgave me a five bob rise in pay. He also, after a week or so, made me into a measuring boy, the lowest rung on the management ladder. Dad, honest socialist that he was, consistently refused invitations to become an official. He didn't want to be one of "them." I changed sides without a qualm. I saw the progression before me, measuring boy, university, shotfirer, deputy, overman, undermanager, manager.

There were three measuring boys in the colliery, one for each coal face. The seam we were working was 5-6 feet thick, sloping at about 25 degrees, the supply road, at the top of the coal face, brought in supplies, mostly pit props, and the bottom road had a belt conveyor to take coal out. The coal face, 100 yards long, ran between the two roads.

The colliery had two shafts. The upcast shaft had a huge fan which sucked 350,000 cubic feet of air a minute around the workings, diluting the amount of coal gas (methane) to negligible proportions.

My coal face had about two dozen colliers, the cream of the miners. Colliers were paid on piece work. The more coal they filled the more money they earned. Colliers earned up to £15 a week. Everyone else got £5 15sa. My first job in the morning was to measure each man's stent and mark it with chalk on the roof. Some colliers wanted 12 feet, some took 15, some only 10. The coal cutter, on the previous night shift, had undercut the coal to a depth of 4ft 6 inches. This is how far the coal face advanced each day.

At the end of the shift I measured the seam thickness in three places in each stent, so that my books showed the length and the average height of each stent. A cubic yard of coal weighs one ton, and every tram from my coal face was marked with the face number and weighed on the surface. So the manager knew exactly how many tons he had raised from my face, and exactly how many tons I had paid for. If I paid for more coal than he had raised I was in for it! The colliers would try and cheat me when I measured. I had to ask the collier to put his thumb in the ring of my tape and hold it to the floor. I could see that he was holding it properly. I had to look up and rub the tape against the roof to measure the thickness. Every single time I could feel the collier turn over his thumb as I looked up, stealing an inch. I could feel the tug. I didn't complain. I just stopped the tape an inch from the roof.

A couple of hours before the end of the shift I'd check how colliers were doing. There was one collier, at the bottom of the face, who only took 10 feet and was never able to finish, on account of his propensity for drinking a lot of cider every evening. I would send a collier who was finished early to help him, give that collier perhaps an extra two feet of pay, and take two feet off the laggard. I also negotiated extra money for additional work, such as a fall of roof or the nuisance of the cutter in his stent. Typically it would be one and sixpence, about seven and a half pence in the new money. It doesn't seem a lot now.

Sometimes, through no fault of the colliers, broken belts, shortage of empties, they were unable to clear their coal. I had to negotiate with them how much money they would be cropped. I'd crop them two feet or three feet or whatever seemed suitable, because men on the afternoon shift had to be paid for clearing the coal, and the only money available to pay them was what I had cropped from the day shift. Only after clearing the day shift coal could they get on with their own work of dismantling the conveyor and re-assembling it in the new track.

There was one occasion when, very early in the shift, a fall of rock took the back of the hand off one collier. He was patched up and sent out, but I couldn't pay him for any coal because I had to pay other colliers to clear his stent. I was criticised by some men for that. He'd been underground for a couple of hours and got no pay for it. But the other colliers who cleared his stent could have given him a couple of feet if they were so inclined. The colliers' take home pay was dependant on how much they could wheedle out of me. If this seemed like a lot of responsibility for a boy of 16, I didn't feel it.

The coal face had a steel conveyor, the Westphalia Retarder (we called it a Hitler), made in Germany. It's astonishing to think that Germany, by 1948, was exporting machinery, after having all its factories and 75 per cent of its houses destroyed during the war. There were long periods when the Hitler was on stop. A journey of empty trams would be brought to the end of the main road conveyor, the conveyor would start up, colliers would be frantically shovelling onto the Hitler until the journey was full and had to be changed. The stationary Hitler didn't stop the colliers shovelling coal onto it. By the time the new empty journey was ready the Hitler was buried and wouldn't start. So all hands on deck to free it and start again.

On the way out I had to count the number of full and empty trams I passed on the way to pit bottom and report to the manager. He wanted to know how much coal winding he needed to do on the afternoon shift, to ensure there were enough empties available for the next morning.

I had other jobs to do. Collecting dust sample was one. The law required the manager to spread incombustible stone dust in the roadways, to reduce the coal dust's ability to explode in the case of a gas explosion. The samples had to show less than 50 per cent coal, and I had to collect it in a prescribed way, some from the floor, some from the shoulders of the arches supporting the roof, some from the sides. The samples were sent to a lab for analysis. My first samples, carefully collected, didn't pass the test, and I had a roasting from the manager. "If it looks too black, throw a handful of stone dust in the sample," he told me, i.e., fake the sample!

Saturday was a short shift, an hour less. It was also an optional shift for the miners, and not all chose to work it. Not all coal faces were working, so no shortage of empties! Dad was a collier, but normally didn't work on my coal face, for obvious reasons, but one Saturday he did. I had to be back up the pit by 9 am to give the measurements to the clerks who had to work out the money for the colliers. So I had to leave the coal face by 8.30.

We got to the face by 7.30, I measured the stents and the heights by 7.45. Dad had taken his usual 15 feet. He threw me a shovel. "Let's see what you're made of," he said. We both shovelled furiously. We didn't put up any timber yet, we just shovelled coal, and by 8.30, when I had to leave, we had cleared all his coal, 15 tons of it. I think I passed the test!

We had no pit head baths, and at home we had no bath room. We had a tin bath on the floor in front of the kitchen fire, on which we boiled the kettle. Dad washed his top half first (not his back). I washed my top half, kneeling at the tub. Then we went out while Dad washed his bottom half, then it was my turn. The water was black by then. We didn't wash our backs until the weekend.

At the Friday dance in the Bomb and Dagger it was said that you could always tell the girls who danced with a miner.

Llanharan girls would slip a hand under the boy's shirt to stroke his back, then wipe her sweaty brow with her hand, leaving the tell-tale coal dust on the face.

An old miner ready for work.

The Lover

You can't become a true lover. It's not something you can achieve. You are either born a lover or you are not. It's like being tall or being born in Wales. You can't boast about it. It's not like passing exams. It's a natural state. Lovers lead a happy life because of that state. It always turns out for the best for them. Something bad happens, but then something better than before happens. This blessed state is rare, but John Thomas had it.

He lived up at the Huts with his family, his wife Sally and their three children. She was round as a button, but he was so proud of her. When he came down to the village with her he would present her to people as if she were a Queen. "This is my Sally. Isn't she beautiful?"

He worked down the pit, nights regular, as a haulage driver. On the night shift he was rarely required to do any actual work. He was just there in case he was needed. He just sat there in the warm and thought about his Sally. He worked only four shifts a week. When the five day week came in miners were paid six days pay for five days work, but only if they worked all five shifts. If they lost a shift they also lost the bonus payment. That fifth day was called a *doubler*. It was worth two day's pay. So John Thomas, working only four shifts a week was paid only two thirds of a week's pay, less that £4 a week. When the manager asked him why he worked only four shifts a week he said it was because he couldn't live on three day's pay.

On his Friday off he came down to the village with his Sally for the weekly shop, and when that was done he popped into the Eagle for a drink. He was the most contented man

I ever knew.

Malvolio Humphrey was a man of private means. He was an avid collector of curiosities. He wasn't very good at it, but he was very assiduous. His house was full of knick-knacks of not much value, but which had caught his attention. If it was old it was probably valuable, he thought. He lived alone and travelled widely, following his hobby.

I don't know why he came to the Brynna, but come he did, on a Friday afternoon. The village didn't strike him as being of much interest, just a long strip of poor houses and a pub. But you never knew. Some of those houses could have something in the attic they cared nothing for, but which might interest him. He went into the Eagle for a drink.

Elsie May the landlady was a tidy little woman. She cared about her purse, her customers and her husband, in that order. She spotted Malvolio Humphrey as a wealthy man as soon as he came in. "If I'd known you were coming I'd have lit a fire in the snug" she said. "That's quite alright Madam" he said, "I'll be perfectly happy in the bar". She glowed. A perfect gentleman, she thought.

John Thomas was in the bar drinking with No-Good-Boyo and Beau Davies. They were laughing and joking as men do when they are on their own. Beau Davies said "let's drink a toast to all the girls we have loved. I drink to all the shop girls in Pencoed except those over the age of 30". No-Good Boyo said "I drink to Lana Turner". Neither of the other two believed he had even met Lana Turner, let alone loved her. John Thomas said " I drink to my Sally, the most beautiful woman in the world"

Malvolio Humphrey had spotted a bed warmer that Elsie May had bought in a jumble sale for half a crown. It had a round brass box for the hot coals and a long wooden handle.

She thought it would look good on the pub wall. Malvolio Humphrey wanted to buy it, and after some haggling gave Elsie £10 for it.

John Thomas saw this going on and said "I've got an antique back home". Malvolio asked him what it was. John said, "it's a kind of tea pot my grandfather brought back. He was a soldier, served in India. I remember him talking about a spot of bother he sorted out on the Kyber Pass. Then he went to China, something to do with opium, I think. He brought back this tea pot thing. It's painted metal, the kids use it for pretend tea parties"

Malvolio Humphrey tried to hide his growing excitement. He knew exactly what it was. It was a 2000 year old tea pot used by the old Emperors of China. There were very few surviving, and each was worth thousands of pounds.

"Would you be interested in selling it?" He asked.

"I don't know. The kids like it, and it IS of sentimental value"

"Can I just see it then?"

"Yes of course, if you can come along home with me"

"I'll give you a lift in my car"

"That's very nice of you" said John Thomas, " but the track up to the Huts is not much more than a foot path. Can't get a car up there".

Malvolio Humphrey took his bed warmer and walked out of the Eagle with John Thomas. They walked across to Aaron David's shop and looked in the window. "I wanted to buy the kids a few sweets and things, but the money didn't stretch that far this week" said John. Malvolio saw a way to ingratiate himself. "Please allow me to buy some sweets for your children" he said. They bought some sweets and some playthings, which Malvolio insisted on carrying, along with his bed warmer. The draper's shop next door had a blue satin dress in the window. John Thomas sighed. "I was going to buy that dress for my Sally. She's set her heart on it, but I couldn't afford it. It's her birthday today, too."

"I would be delighted to buy that dress as a present for your dear wife" said Malvolio. He was actually more delighted that they were now thoroughly indebted to him, and would be obliged to sell the tea pot to him. Miss Dendle tied up the dress in a nice parcel with a ribbon, and Malvolio insisted on carrying that too.

He was quite loaded now. He took off his belt (his braces had to suffice to hold up his trousers) and tied the bed warmer onto his back. His arms were full and the pan of the bed warmer bumped against his calves as he walked. The track up to the Huts was long and rough, but not as rough as the Huts themselves.

They had been built long ago as homes for workers at the brickworks there. It was such a big operation that a two mile full gauge railway had been built from the brickworks to the Swansea/ London railway line. The Huts were primitive, no electricity, no running water, no toilets, I heard. Only poor people lived there and people hiding from the Police. The brickworks had long gone, and the railway line torn up and taken away.

By the time the little party arrived Malvolio Humphrey was just about worn out. Sally Thomas was gracious. She was so pleased to receive the dress and the children were delighted with their presents. Mrs Thomas offered a cup of tea, "Where's grandad's tea pot, my love" asked John. "I do believe it's out in the garden" said Sally, "I'll go and find it".

It was quite a long time before she returned, and Malvolio

Humphrey was getting more and more anxious. He almost grabbed the tea pot from her, and looked inside it for any markings. There were markings on the bottom, but they were almost obscured by years of tannin.

"May I ask, Mrs Thomas, if you have any bicarbonate of soda, or something similar, to clean off this tannin?" "Yes of course Sir" said Sally, I'll see to it now". They sat, the Thomases happily and Malvolio Humphrey impatiently, while the bicarbonate did its work.

By now it was getting dusk, and with no electricity they had to use a candle to peer inside the pot. The writing on the bottom became clear as they blinked in the dim light. It said, "Property of the War Office".

The Funeral of Thomas Magoo

Magoo was dead.

Mrs Magoo planned to give him a funeral with a bit of class. She was, after all, the daughter of a High Court judge - almost a Lord Lieutenant, in the county of Pembrokeshire, Little England beyond Wales, an English speaking county surrounded by Welsh speaking Carmarthenshire and Cardiganshire

She was properly brought up, learned to ride and say grace in Latin before meals. She was one of the first women in Wales, at 17, to have her own motor cycle. She was prepared for a fine marriage.

Then she met Thomas Magoo, a Cardigan man. Thomas wooed her and wed her and moved East to seek his fortune. He ended up in the Brynna and worked in Brynna Wood colliery. He didn't earn a fortune there. He earned a nickname. He was caught stealing a piece of cheese out of another man's Tommybox and was named "Mouse". The name stuck and over time took on an affectionate tone. His son Hugo was named Little Mouse.

Cardiganshire men are renowned for their parsimony. If a man peels an orange underground the ventilation takes the smell of the orange all around the workings, and all the miners in the vicinity clamour for a segment. A Cardiganshire man is the only man who can peel an orange in his trouser pocket, so avoiding the orange smell escaping and keeping the orange to himself.

And now he was dead.

Mrs Magoo was a tall handsome woman with iron grey

hair. She was fond of hyperbole. Some said that her father wasn't a judge at all, but merely a clerk to the court. She was effusive about her friends, giving them achievements they did not have. "She's a wonderful seamstress," "She's a high quality pastry cook." Then, an hour later, talking disparagingly about them.

She had invited everybody who was anybody in the Brynna to come back to her house for refreshments after the internment. She had brought out her home made wine and bought some sweet sherry for the ladies. She had even invited the toffee-nosed Imelda Cousins and her daughter Camilla, even though they would cut her dead when they met in the street. Imogen Edwards, her neighbour, had run around producing tit-bits to eat, and had spent the whole morning, while others were attending the funeral, preparing and cooking chips. There was a great pile of chips available when guests trooped in. None of the most important people had turned up, not even Imogen Cousins and especially not Mr Thomas the Water Board.

Mrs Magoo held court, talking brightly, offering food and drink. "Do have a few chips." "Can I offer you a glass of my Elderflower wine?" Her Elderflower wine was lethal. Big Gwyn had arrived early and made straight for it. Mrs Magoo was praising her her late husband. "Mr Magoo," she said, "was a very sociable man."

Big Gwyn agreed, "He could certainly put the drink away."

"He did drink a little, and sometimes too much. But it was because he was led astray by the wrong sort of men," she said, glaring at Big Gwyn.

"Some thought I was perhaps too strict with him, but it was for his own good. If I hadn't taken care of him like that he would have been drunk all the time"

Mrs Magoo's day was saved when Peter Evans arrived. Peter was a student at the university, preparing to be a famous professor in the future.

"I'm so glad you came, Mr Evans," she said. "Do come and sit next to me. It's so nice to have some intelligent conversation. Just look at Mrs Blower over there. She knows we're talking about her, but she's deaf as a post, can't hear a word."

She barely recognised Mr Bronowski, who had also been running around, moving furniture, lighting fires, fetching and carrying. He was a Pole, barely 5 feet 4 inches tall. Mrs Magoo was a tidy bit taller than him. He was one of those foreigners who had escaped to Britain for a better life. The Poles had always suffered. At one time Poland disappeared. The Russians and the Germans had carved up Poland between them. And the Polish Jews, for he was one, suffered more than most.

But he had that tenacity of spirit, common to all those who flee from tyrants, which made polyglot Britain a nation to be feared. Wellington once said of his troops, "I don't know if they frighten the French, but they put the fear of God into me".

When Mr Magoo died, Mrs Magoo had been visiting her parents in Haversfordwest. Hugo had stayed with his father.

Mr Magoo had been ailing for a long time. He had called Dr Pat. "Be straight with me, Dr Pat. I'm feeling really bad. How long have I got?"

Dr Pat pursed his lips, "Your liver is shot to pieces. I think you'll be gone by the morning. Is there anything you'd like me to do for you?"

Magoo did have a major problem, but he didn't think Dr Pat could help. He had not long received an anonymous letter , telling him that his wife had been having an affair with that little Pole Bronowski for the last fourteen years, and he would find evidence of this in Mrs Magoo's sewing bag. He was looking at it now, letters from Bronowski to his wife, little love tokens. There was no doubt about it. How could she have deceived him for all these years, after all he had done for her? And with a Pole too! Was his beloved Hugo his own son even? He dispaired. What could he do in the few hours remaining to him to avenge himself on both of them?

The funeral party, as always when strong drink was involved, got acrimonious. Imogen Edwards didn't think she was properly appreciated and said so to Big Gwyn. Big Gwyn egged her on until Mrs Magoo was obliged to remind her that she was the daughter of a High Court judge, almost a Lord Lieutenant, and would not be spoken to like that.

Two more Poles arrived, uninvited. One of them, who had a stutter as well as a foreign accent, had a shouting match with deaf old Mrs Blower. The noise level was rising. Then Mr Thomas the Water Board turned up, thank goodness. He took charge, separated the warring parties, made a little speech praising Mouse Magoo as a welcome addition to the village, and peace was restored.

It was barely three months later that Mrs Magoo, throwing off her widow's weeds, graciously consented to marry Bronowski. Bronowski seemed bent on taking over Little Mouse's role as man of the house. He started giving Hugo orders. Hugo, even at 12 years of age, was taller then Bronowski. He said to him "I don't want you to marry my mother. You are to leave my house immediately and never come back".

Bronowski was in the habit, when annoyed, of using expletives in Polish, and he did so now. He told Hugo that when he, Bronowski was master of the house, Hugo would have to mend his manners.

At that time all men had a revolver in the house. Hugo fetched the revolver, put it against Bronowski's forehead and pulled the trigger. Mrs Magoo fluttered. "He was a Count in his native land, a Von. I would have been Lady Von Bronowski. My breast would have been covered with jewels. I am, after all, the daughter of a judge."

She couldn't understand why Hugo had killed her intended, so he told her, quite calmly. "Before Dad died he told me that Bronowski was his enemy and your enemy and that I should protect you from him. You'd better tell the police that Bronowski killed himself when you told him that you would not marry him."

The Christmas Tree

Brynna was a working class village. When the Brynna bypass was built, taking the road from Bridgend to Cardiff away from the village, Brynna slumped a little more. Most people rented, many let out rooms. There were only three cars in the village, and three private telephones, Brynna 1, Brynna 2 and Brynna 3.

There was plenty of low paid work available during the war, even seasonal work for children. The old age pension was only ten bob a week. I don't know what the widow's pension was, but Mrs Smith, living a few doors from us in Southall Street, was struggling. She had only girls in the house. Her husband had died from some wasting disease.

We had a load (a ton) of coal delivered to our back lane once a month. Dad would put it away in our coal cwtch, but he always took a couple of buckets of coal to Mrs Smith. I think other miners did the same.

We were looking forward to the Christmas festivities. Dad was earning good money, and even though we were five children by then, we were comparatively well off. Certainly better off than Mrs Smith, who couldn't even afford to buy a Christmas tree. I was quite disturbed about that. Then I remembered a story Aunty Rene had told me about her brother, our Dad.

It was the late 1920s. Dad was a teenager. He had eight siblings, including Ronald, 6 or 8 years old and sickly. (He died during the war of heart disease, aged 21.). They were still in the Great Depression following the general strike of 1926.

They couldn't afford to buy a Christmas tree. Dad, the oldest boy, wouldn't countenance that. He took a spade and walked the few miles to Ewenny, where he dug up a Christmas tree and carried it home. He was too honest to steal it. He was only borrowing it. After Christmas he carried it back to Ewenny and replanted it. I thought we should do the same for Mrs Smith.

The Forestry Commission had taken over huge areas of mountain for planting fir trees. I knew it well. I had worked there planting saplings on a piece work basis. The theory was that by planting in succession, by the time the last ones were planted the first ones were ready for felling and new saplings planted in their place. I had it in mind that they were for pit props, previously obtained from Norway. I wasn't quite big enough to manage the job on my own so I sought help.

Granville Hawkes was a year or two older than me, and that much bigger and stronger. Later on we played football together for the Brynna. He was a centre forward, I was a centre half. I like to think that I invented the sweeper centre half system later taken up by professional clubs.

Granville Hawkes (we called him Obie) lived across the road from me. I knocked on his door.

"Is Obie in?" I asked.

"Who's Obie?" Asked his father.

"Obie 'Awkes," I said, "Is he in?"

He called him and I explained what I wanted to do. He was all for it, and together we went up to the Forestry Commission to borrow a Christmas tree.

Having worked there I knew the area quite well. I knew where to hide. I knew where the wide paths were between individual plantations. I guessed the paths were wide in order to accommodate the lorries to carry away the logs after felling. We kept a sharp lookout for Forestry wardens, and crept about quietly, like wraiths. We got away with it. We considered the risk of returning the tree after Christmas, but we decided we had to follow the plan that had worked in 1928.

Mrs Smith had tears in her eyes when we brought her the tree, She pressed us to her meagre bosom. She fully understood the need to return it after Christmas. I have to say it gave Granville and me a warm glow as well, and cemented our friendship. It was what the Americans might call a "special relationship."

I moved away, and we lost touch. I was in my mid-eighties when I had an attack of nostalgia. While I was still able to drive I wanted to see the Brynna again, see the football pitch where I had twinkle-toed along the touchline, see the house where I was born.

I remembered a poem Mam had taught me:

> I remember, I remember the house where I was born,
>
> The little window where the sun came peeping in each morn.
>
> It never came a wink too soon
>
> Nor brought too long a day
>
> But now I often wish the night had borne my breath away.

I wanted to see my old pals again. I planned a grand tour, see the Brynna, call in for lunch with Ron Sumption, my university pal, who lived near Cardiff, in Peterstone -Super-Ely. After we graduated he didn't spend much time in the coal industry. He got a job with a publisher in The Haymarket in

London, and paid £5000 for a house in Epsom. Ten years later I paid £5000 for a house in Hayward's Heath.

We had a nice lunch. Sumption brought out the papers we had sat for our finals. I couldn't, after all that time, understand the questions, let alone consider the answers.

And, of course, I wanted to see how Obie Hawkes was doing. He was living in Llanharry, near our Joe, who arranged for me to go to Granville's house for a cup of tea. I feared how I would find him, but was delighted with his appearance. He was straight and robust, dignified, not much changed from his centre forward days. He spoke well, his house was very nice, well furnished and spotlessly clean. We talked of football, of our successes and failures. We had won the Bridgend and District Senior Open Cup in 1955. I have my trophy still. We chuckled about our borrowing the Christmas tree and getting away with it. I told him about where I was living then, on the South Coast of England. I felt so good about him, and he looked so well, that I said he and his wife should come and visit. I would put them up and show them around Portsmouth and Southampton and Bournemouth and the seaside resorts close at hand. "It's only two and a half hours away by car, Granville, and it's motorway and dual carriageway almost all the way. Easy driving".

"I haven't got a car," he said. "I never passed my driving test."

That set me back on my heels. But worse was to come. He didn't have a passport. He'd never been abroad. I felt ineffably sad. Here was this fine man, a man as good as me if not better. Yet I had travelled the world, all over Europe, North and South America, the Middle East, all over the Pacific area, Hong Kong, China, Singapore, Jakarta, Bali, Kuala Lumpur, Bangkok, Phillipines, I had stayed in the world's best hotels, eaten in the world's best restaurants. All this and more. And what was the difference between Granville and me? The 11 Plus. I went to Grammar School and he didn't. Rich people send their children to private schools . Grammar Schools allowed poor children to escape from poverty, lead a more fulfilling life. Life isn't fair.

I hadn't known his wife. She held her left arm awkwardly, as if she had had a stroke. She was quiet, She let us talk. Granville said to her "Would you make us some tea darling?" And again, "Do you need any help sweetheart?" And, "Do you want to come and join us my lovely?"

I said, "It's astonishing. You've been married, what, 60 years?"

"Sixty-two," he said.

"Sixty-two years, and you still address her with endearments. That's really lovely"

"It's not quite like that, John" he said, "Fact is, I don't always remember her name"

The Coal Wagon

Morgan Morgan was the same age as me, a friend who lived in William Street. As a boy he had his tonsils out, and the doctor managed to damage one of his vocal chords. That vocal chord hung limp and spastic, the other remained firm and plump.

As a result his voice was hoarse. He sounded like an old man whose voice had been ruined by years of cigars and whiskey. It was very useful for our school plays where he was always cast in the role of an old man. A little later, when we were in our back yard playing with our bikes, I managed to catch his calf between the bike chain and the drive wheel, which took a sizeable chunk out of his calf. After that in our school plays he took the part of an old man with a limp.

Although it was entirely my fault, I never got the blame for his leg, even from Morgan who of course was there at the time. I know that because very many years later a friend of mine from North Wales met Morgan on a cruise, and Morgan told my friend that he remembered me with affection.

The GWR railway line ran between the allotments and Brynna Wood. Morgan and I, now teenagers, crossed the railway line and climbed the embankment into Brynna Wood, where we came upon a distressing scene. Miss Dendle, the draper, was being harangued by a man on a magnificent chestnut hunter. The horse must have been 16 or 17 hands.

It seems that Miss Dendle had taken her billhook to Brynna Wood to cut a few runner bean sticks. She had tied them up and was carrying them home when the horseman accosted her. Miss Dendle was twice our age, but no bigger than us. She had a neat little figure, more wiry than slim. As a young flapper she had aspirations. She had dreamed of going to Europe, to Paris and San Tropez. She had saved enough money when Mr Hitler put a spoke in the wheel.

Foreign travel was out for the duration. Now she had reached that age when single women think, "Will it ever happen to me? Is it too late? Am I still in with a chance?"

Miss Dendle was holding on to her bean sticks. She was looking very dejected. We said "What's going on here?"

The man said, "It's none of your business, but you're not allowed to cut bean sticks in this wood. I'm going to confiscate them."

I said, "No you're not". I moved to the front of the horse, reached up and took hold of the bridle. I pulled the horse's head down to my chest. That horse was going nowhere.

Morgan moved to the opposite corner of the horse. The rider didn't know whether to look at Morgan or at me. We must have seemed quite menacing. Underneath that veneer of Grammar School civilisation we were Brynna boys still, and nobody messed with Brynna boys.

Morgan said, in that old man's voice of his, "This is Brynna Wood. We've always cut bean sticks here and will continue to do so."

The man said "I'll have the law on you".

Morgan said "My name is Morgan Morgan." He paused. "If you cause me any trouble you'll find you'll get a lot of bad luck. And it won't be only me after you. It'll be the whole of the Brynna. Now clear off out of our wood, and stop molesting helpless women." He laid the flat of the billhook on the man's thigh for emphasis.

With that he gave me the nod. I released the horse's head, Morgan gave the horse a resounding slap on the withers, and away bounded horse and rider. We never saw hide nor hair of them thereafter.

Miss Dendle was almost weeping with relief. We were her heroes. We walked with her back down the embankment. There was a double rail track at that point, one track a siding, and on the siding was a train of empty coal wagons. Miss Dendle, still nervous, asked us what it was doing there. We explained. The wagons were waiting to go to Llanharan colliery. The manager didn't want the wagons on colliery property too early because the GWR charged a rent, called demurrage, on empty coal wagons. So they were kept on the siding until the last minute.

It's worth noting that when a colliery is sunk it needs three things close at hand, a railway, electric power at 33,000 volts, and a river. Why a river? I'll tell you. Coal comes up the pit and is taken to a coal preparation plant. The coal is tipped onto a slowly moving steel conveyor belt. Men standing on each side of it remove any pieces of stone. The clean coal goes onto a shaking screen, with holes in it. The larger pieces of coal go to the end of the screen and into a wagon. The rest drops onto another screen with smaller holes, and so on. Soon all the coal is sorted into their sizes, grains, peas, beans, cobbles etc. The smallest coal, dust plus stone particles goes into the washery for separation. That is what the river is for. The coal dust/ stone mixture is agitated in water, the heavier stone goes to the bottom, the lighter coal rises to the surface and is sucked onto a vacuum drum and scraped off. I don't know why we bothered. It's a poor quality fuel. It is of little value. It can't be used in closed stoves or on open fires, but it's just about acceptable in power stations. Colliery managers, for some reason, are obsessed with the percentage of coal left in the tailings. They brag about it or they are ashamed of it. Three per cent they are ashamed. Two per cent they brag about it. A manager's life is not always rewarding.

All the used water from the washery goes back into the river. The river water is black. The banks of the river are black.

Miss Dendle seemed interested in the wagons. She seemed fascinated by Morgan's Humphrey Bogart voice. He said to her, "Have you ever seen the inside of a wagon, Miss Dendle?" She said she hadn't and asked if it was interesting. Now the outside of a coal wagon is quite interesting. It has a long handle to activate the brake, and the couplings are very heavy. But the inside is no more interesting than an empty shoe box. But Morgan said, "I think you'll find it interesting."

There was nothing for it but for Morgan to clamber up the side of the wagon, hang over it and hold out his hand to help Miss Dendle up. I tried to help from below, and with a pull and a push and a brief flash of thigh Miss Dendle was in the coal wagon with Morgan Morgan.

I kept watch outside, ready to tap on the side of the wagon with the billhook in case of alarm. After about 15 minutes Morgan had finished showing her the inside of the wagon and they clambered out.

They were a curiously matched pair, Morgan with his old man's voice and Miss Dendle with her wiry figure. It was touching.

They were a bit dusty. Morgan gave Miss Dendle his handkerchief to clean up. It wasn't a real handkerchief, just a piece of cloth torn from an old bed sheet. Morgan called it his "snot rag". She couldn't wet it in the river because it was so black, so she just spat on it, and was passably clean by the time we all trooped home. If it was a romance it didn't last long. Before she had finished picking her runner beans Miss Dendle left the village. Gone to work in a hotel in Switzerland, we were told. That job didn't last long either. Miss Dendle returned to the draper's shop. She looked a little chastened, but she no longer had that "*Will it ever happen?*" *look*.

The Miners' Fortnight

Just after I graduated, in 1952, I met Jack Jones. He was a lampman at Wyndham colliery in Nantymoel, nearing retirement. He was a wonderful raconteur and I admired him greatly. I wished I could tell a tale as well as he did. I improved a bit over the years but never reached his class.

He told me that when he was a young man, around the time of the First World War, he became friendly with an old man who was an official of the South Wales Federation of Mineworkers (the Fed). The Fed was formed in 1898 to look after the interests of miners, ex-miners and the widows of miners. My grandfather, Tommy (Yorke) Evans was the first treasurer of the Fed. The first secretary was William Brae and the first president was William Abraham MP. At first membership was voluntary, but soon it was mandatory. Every miner had to join the Fed except colliery officials and managers, who had their own unions.

Jack Jones told me that he attended a meeting of the Fed, sitting at the knee of this Federation old man. The old man put forward a proposal that mine owners should provide paid holidays for miners. After the meeting Jack said to him, "Were you really serious, asking for holidays with pay?"

"It may not happen in my lifetime, boyo, but it will in yours," the old man answered.

And so it came to pass. It resulted in the Miners' Fortnight. Every colliery in South Wales closed for the same two weeks in August, and the miners received holiday pay for it.

For the local seaside resorts, Barry and Porthcawl, it was like Christmas. Thousands of miners and their families descended on them by train and by motor coach. Few miners could afford to go away for a fortnight or even a week. It was all day trips. The railway was like a magnet to me. I recall us all walking to Llanharan and standing on the platform waiting for the train to Porthcawl. With a great roar and a hissing the train would pull in, making a vacuum, and I could feel myself being sucked towards it. Dad had to hold my hand tightly to prevent it.

Both Porthcawl and Barry had great fun fairs. Both had extensive sands to get lost on. It was a dress-up day for grownups. Mam even wore her pearls.

Dad wore his flat cap and a collar and tie. We kids wore our woolen bathers and made sand castles. Tizer and Dandelion and Burdock were consumed. Sand got in the sandwiches. I believe some of the men may have called in for a beer or two. In any case, when we went by motor coach we invariably stopped at a quiet spot on the road, and the men would rush out and stand against the bus to spend a penny. And also invariably, when the men were at their most vulnerable, the bus would pull away a few yards to the shrieks of the women on the bus.

The motor coaches were arranged by a local company and it wasn't just the miners who went along. The whole village joined in, even people who were quite well off.

Jack Lewis was quite well off. He was a Brynna boy who had done well. He had worked for himself since leaving school, and at 27 he had a thriving hatter's business. He lived in the Brynna, but had a manufactory in Bridgend. Dad bought one of his bowler hats, size seven and three eighths, same size as me.

Mollie has it now.

But Jack, by his attention to business, had missed all the growing up that teenagers learned. He never went on Sunday walks on that road between Llanharan and Talbot Green. It was for young teens, boys walked on one side of the road, girls on the other. They just looked at one another. There was no talking to them or touching them. That came in the later teens. Jack was naive. It wasn't that he didn't like girls, he just didn't know what to do about it.

He was good company, always laughing and joking, but no girls could get near him.

Marion Lewis (no relation) came to the Brynna when her mother was left a legacy, a house and a modest amount of money. There were some pretty girls in the village, but Marion, at 17, outshone them all. The young girls didn't like her because their boy friends were ogling her, but Marion didn't encourage them, and was of such a sunny disposition that everyone came to like her.

Both Jack and Marion, with her mother, were on the coach to Porthcawl. Apart from the beach and the fun fair, Porthcawl had the Welsh version of the Lanes in Brighton, curiosity shops, boutiques, antiques and the like. Marion and her mother came across a window in which was a beautiful porcelain vase, decorated with country scenes, lambs, leopards, deer, coloured birds, blue skies, flowers. It looked like Paradise. Other day trippers came to look, it was so wonderful. It was priced at £50. No-one carried that kind of money in their pockets and in any case, few could afford it.

Jack Lewis could. The following day he went to Porthcawl again. He bought the vase, put it in a box and wrote on it "To

Marion with love".

He got off the bus in Brynna and saw a Dolau boy in the Square. He could tell it was a Dolau boy, he was walking around in circles. Jack shouted at him.

"Oi! Do you know where Marion Lewis lives? I'll give you five bob to take this box to her home and give it to Marion. But I don't want you to tell anyone, anyone at all, who gave it to you."

The boy walked off with the box and was intercepted by Pete the Spy. Pete was an overman at the colliery, the most senior of under-official jobs. He would never be a colliery manager but he was well set up. He had also fallen for Marion but he had two disadvantages. He was old, 40, and he had a huge nose, like Jimmy Durante. He was often referred to as Jimmy, but only behind his back.

He said to the Dolau boy, "Where are you going with that box?"

"I'm taking it to Marion Lewis."

"Who did you get it from?"

"I'm sorry, I'm not allowed to tell you that, it's a secret."

Pete the Spy asked him, "Who told you to keep it a secret?"

He said, "Jack Lewis".

Pete the Spy said, "You're very good to keep a secret like that. But I'm going up that way. I can drop it off at Marion's house for you."

Pete the Spy stopped at the house. Marion and her mother were in the garden.

Pete said, "I have brought a present for you, and I leave it at your feet together with my heart."

Marion said, "I want neither your present nor your heart. Take both away." Marion's mother told Pete the Spy to leave the box and come back in a month. She was sure that Marion would warm to him.

When Marion unpacked the box she was delighted to see the vase inside. Her mother insisted that twice a week Marion should go to the spring to fill it with water and pick wild flowers to put in it. Only the finest water for the finest vase in the Brynna! Marion would go really early to the spring, and now she found there, each time, a lovely bouquet of flowers with a note, "For the lovely Marion." Both she and her mother thought they were from Pete the Spy.

Jack met her one morning as she was leaving the spring, "Let me carry your vase for you," he said. They arrived at Marion's house at the same time as Pete the Spy. "Have a care with that vase," he shouted, "If you break it you'll have to replace it; it cost me £150."

"No it didn't," said Jack, "I paid £50 for that vase in Porthcawl in the Miner's Fortnight, and sent it to Marion as a present."

Marion said, "Did you really, Jack? I thought you didn't care about me. You never approached me. You never asked me for a dance at the Bomb and Dagger."

"I have loved you from the moment I first saw you, but was too shy. And I thought I was too old for you. So I bought the vase for you. I grew these flowers in my own garden for you. I worshipped you from afar."

There were tears in Marion's eyes. All her dreams had come true. She told him that she loved him and that she would care for him always. They were married in St. Peter's Church. She didn't even have to change her surname.

She just moved from Miss Marion Lewis to Mrs Marion Lewis. They had a very happy life together. They were not blessed with children. When Jack died Marion presented the vase to the Welsh Folk Museum at St.Fagan's. You can see it there today, on the reception desk, filled twice a week with fresh flowers.

PC 49

It has to be said that it wasn't a great start for PC 49 Alexander Wass. After his initial training and his posting to the Portsmouth City Police he never in his worst nightmares imagined that he would be banished to a beat in the Brynna.

It was all the fault of The Lord Chamberlain, really, for introducing the decency laws in the theatre. The law had been quite clear. No nudity on stage. Then nudity was allowed provided that the girls didn't move a muscle, and the Police were deputed to make sure of that.

PC A Wass was assigned to the Theatre Royal in Portsmouth. He was to stay in the wings and monitor what was going on on stage. What was going on was quite tasteful. A new moon swung to and fro over the stage. Lying on the new moon was a comely young lady with no clothes on and not moving a muscle. On the stage itself were a number of representations of fluffy clouds, flimsy cardboard cut-outs, supported by a brace to keep them upright.

PC 49 A Wass, keenly aware of his duties, had crept out from the wings until he was hiding behind a cloud directly beneath the young lady on the new moon. He was watching carefully for any muscle movements when he inadvertently knocked over the cloud which concealed him from the audience. The audience was entranced by the sight of a lanky young Police Officer on his hands and knees looking up at the flanks of a comely young lady.

He panicked.

Not only was he spotted by the wildly cheering audience,

he was also spotted by his Chief Superintendent who was doing his own monitoring duties from the comfort of the stalls.

Poor old PC 49 could have treated the the whole affair nonchalantly. He could have stood up, whistled cheerfully and sauntered off stage. Instead he turned around, remained on his hands and knees and crawled into the anonymity of the wings.

It was quite embarrassing for the Chief Constable. He wanted it to disappear, which meant making PC49 A Wass disappear. He called an old mate, the Chief Constable of Glamorgan, to ask if he could take Wass off his hands. His old mate wanted to know exactly why he wanted his officer transferred and the Portsmouth Chief told him, after extracting a promise of absolute confidentiality. It wouldn't do if the Portsmouth citizens learned that he had dismissed Wass, now something of a folk hero, to the wilds of Wales.

The Police Force is unique among all the services in that there is no officer class. Everyone starts as a PC, so there is no Old Boy network. The Chief Constable of Glamorgan felt that he had to share his secret with his senior officers. Before poor old Wass even arrived in the village everyone in the Brynna knew everything about him, down to the colour of his eyelashes.

Small boys who had seen Portsmouth Football Club play at Cardiff City learned the Portsmouth chant and greeted their new PC with it at every opportunity, "Play up Pompey, Play up Pompey".

Alexander Wass had been brought up in Titchfield, a village near Portsmouth. He lived with his father, an admiral and his mother, a scion of the Earl Grey Tea family, in a big house with a large garden. He had attended the private school there, West Hill Park, where he had learned to ride and to play cricket. All this made it more frustrating for Wass to be living in a terraced house in William Street in far away Brynna.

Aunty Betty came to his rescue. There is an Aunty Betty in every Welsh village. They are all alike - middle aged, childless and either widowed or married to very quiet husbands. Aunty Betty has access to every house in the village.

She came into our house. She was talking to my mother, but she was addressing me. "That Mr Wass is a very nice young man, and we should be making him welcome. He's only 23 and far from home. He needs us and we need him as a friend. If he catches you scrumping apples it's better if he gives you a clip around the ear than take you to court."

Aunty Betty was his introduction to society. He joined the Llanharan Cricket Club. He was a decent bat, coming in at four or five. He was an excellent fielder, fielding close to the wicket. He took some spectacular one-handed catches at silly mid off.

Brynna wasn't a hotbed of crime. The most exciting thing he had to do was to give Boyo Smith a clip around the ear when he caught him scrumping apples at Annie Owen the Rent's.

He bought himself a car, a 1928 Lagonda. It wasn't new and it wasn't really a car. It was a hearse sold to him by the local undertaker, Jones the Death. The bodywork was beautiful, and when he had taken out the slides it looked like a two seater car with an extra large boot. It was chain driven and had a top speed of 40mph.

He couldn't drink in the Eagle in Brynna, but used the High Corner in Llanharan, where his accent allowed him into the company of the Young Farmers' Club, who met there.

It was in the High Corner that he met Sonia Sandfields. Sonia lived in the Brynna, but thought herself a cut above everyone else. She worked as a window dresser in Howells in Cardiff. She was very good looking but not a very nice person. She rather liked the appellation SS applied to her. When Alexander first spoke to her she gave him a withering look and said, "You can't afford me."

One Friday night at stop tap, when they came out of the High Corner, it was drizzling with rain. Alexander offered Sonia a lift to the Brynna, which she accepted quite sullenly. He walked around to the offside of the car, opened the door for her and closed it behind her with an expensive sounding clunk. As she relaxed on the leather seat on the way home Alexander, smooth talker that he was, won her attention.

He had an educated Home Counties accent. He talked to her about society in the South of England, of polo at Cowdray Park, of sailing in the Adriatic. She thought perhaps that this young man was a cut above the rest.

He invited Sonia to accompany him on a weekend in Cardiff. There was a show at the New Theatre starring Paul Robson. The plan was to drive up there on the Friday, book into the Park Hotel in separate bedrooms, have dinner in a little Italian place he knew in Newport Road, do the show on Saturday evening and, best of all, on the Saturday morning he would take her to an expensive jeweller where she could choose a piece of jewellery as a gift. Not to be sniffed at, even for Miss Toffee Nose.

So it was that they found themselves at the jeweller's counter. The jeweller brought out some pendants and earrings, all about the £85 mark, but Alexander said "Don't you have anything better than that? What about that necklace in the show case?" The jeweller said, "That necklace, sir, costs

£1000." "Bring it out please" said Alexander, "What about that, my dear?"

Sonia couldn't believe it, but Alexander insisted. "I'll give you a cheque for £1000 now" he said modestly.

The jeweller said, "I won't be able to let you take it away until I've cleared the cheque sir." "That's quite alright. I'll come in on Monday to pick up the necklace. Will that give you enough time?"

On the Monday Alexander walked into the shop. "You've got a nerve coming here" said the jeweller, "That cheque you gave me bounced". "Yes, I know" said Alexander, "I've come to apologise to you, but also to thank you for enabling me to have the best weekend of my life".

Bad Grace

If there was anyone less appropriately named than Billy Grace I would like to meet him. Grace was an uncouth itinerant Irish slob. He'd had brushes with the law more than once and had spent some time inside. He had acquired some limited skills and took on jobs nobody else wanted. He was in digs in Dolau when he heard that they were looking for a bricklayer in Llanharan colliery for a one-off underground job.

They were opening a new coal district and Jim Young the Electrical Engineer wanted a new substation built at its entrance. He wanted to build a substantial three feet wide brick wall ten feet high on three sides, on which would rest railway sleepers, and on those RSJs (rolled steel joists). The brickie was wanted to build the wall on a piece work job-and-finish basis. The work was hard and the pay was not great, but beggars can't be choosers.

It was a nights regular job so that he wouldn't interfere with coal production. Grace lied about his experience to get the job and took on a local teenage lad named David Owen as his labourer. David was a good little kid. He had plans to become a policeman when he was old enough.

After a couple of night's work the overman reported to the colliery manager that Grace was building the wall "at a hell of a lick." Colliery managers live a life of suspicion. If something looks too good to be true it probably is. He took his trusty stick and went down to have a look at the wall.

The "trusty stick" is a walking stick carried only by the manager and under manager. It is like a badge of office, a field marshall's baton. It is slim and has a round knob at the top. The knob is indented with a hole in the top. People will tell you that the hole is used to hang a flame lamp, to lift it up to test for gas above head height. I have never used it for that purpose, nor have I seen anyone else use it for that purpose. I think the hole is formed to hold it in the lathe when the carpenter turns the stick.

My main use of the stick was to warn people when I was approaching, by tap, tap tapping it on the rail as I walked. It's warm and dark in a coal mine, and very easy to fall asleep, especially when you are getting out of bed at half past five in the morning. Falling asleep underground is an offence under the Coal Mines Act 1911 and Regulations Made Thereunder. I didn't want to catch anyone sleeping. It's such a nuisance bringing a prosecution, and it's a harsh punishment for a simple mistake. Therefore tap, tap, tap.

The manager took his stick to the wall. He noticed that a lot of bricks had been used but only one bag of cement had been opened. He put his stick against the wall, and pushed. A brick popped out and fell into the void behind. He got some men to pull down the wall and found that Grace had built a single skin wall and filled the void with loose bricks. No wonder he had completed so much! But worse, in the void they found the body of young David Owen.

It transpired that honest young David had remonstrated with Grace about how he was building the wall. "It's unsafe," he said, "it's going to collapse under the roof pressure and kill somebody."

"That's not my problem." said Grace, "I'll be long gone by then with my money, and if you're wise you'll take your money and say nothing." His lips were flecked with spittle and he threatened David with his hatchet. David, brave little kid, persisted and Grace hit him with the hatchet, killing him on the spot. It's easy to hide blood underground. There's a lot of dust to soak it up.

Grace took off David's cap lamp, threw his body over the wall and bricked him in. At the end of the shift he hid David's cap lamp about his person, and when he got to the lamp room replaced David's cap lamp on the stand and collected David's tally from the book. If it hadn't been for the manager's trusty stick Grace could have got away with it.

The manager put some men to remain at the site and went back to the surface. He contacted the police and local doctor and informed the coal owner's company secretary in Cardiff. He informed the Inspector of Mines. Dr Pat arrived at the same time as PC Wass from the Brynna. Dr Pat confirmed the death and the poor lad's body was borne away. PC Wass took a lot of measurements, took charge of Grace's tools, including the hatchet, and collected David's cap lamp in a paper envelope to check for fingerprints.

PC Wass knew that he would have to inform David's mother, who by now would be frantic. She'd been told he'd come up the pit, but he hadn't arrived home. But Wass also knew that he had to do something about Grace.

"Where will he be now?" He asked the manager. The manager looked at his watch. "He'll be still in bed, but when he wakes up about four o'clock he'll know the game is up and he'll scarper"

"I'll go and pick him up, take him in for questioning," said Wass.

"He's a violent man" said the manager, "Take Charlie Bundy with you." Charlie Bundy was the surface foreman, and a former Welsh heavyweight boxing champion. One of Charlie's jobs was to drive a lorry to the bank in Pontyclun every week to collect the money to pay the wages of the 1000 men working at the pit. Charlie was an imposing presence. Nobody ever tried to rob him.

When Charlie rolled up with PC Wass, Grace was lying in bed, still wearing his wellies. He offered no resistance, and together they took him to the Nick in Bridgend, where he was questioned, charged and locked up pending trial.

PC Wass went down the pit the next morning, before the night shift came out. He spoke to a number of men who had ridden to the surface in the same bond as Grace. None of them remembered seeing David at pit bottom, in the cage, or anywhere on the surface. One had even asked Grace where his boy was and received a surly response.

PC Wass did himself no harm at all. He wrapped up the case so well that he got a commendation from the Chief Constable. He put Brynna on the map really. He had his photograph taken with the manager outside the Eagle Hotel for the Glamorgan Gazette, the Western Mail and the Daily Herald. I've still got a copy of that photograph in my souvenir box.

Grace was found guilty and was hanged in Cardiff. His old Irish mother came over for the funeral and said "He was a good boy, so he was."

The Miracle

After I left university I was put on a two year National Coal Board Directed Practical Training Scheme, and at the same time was studying for my professional and statutory qualifications. One of my tasks was a time and motion study of a new development called Horizon Mining.

Until then roadways were driven in coal seams, following the undulations of the coal. In Horizon Mining roadways were like motorways, dead level and straight, cutting through the inclined coal seams as they went. This had the advantage that the main roadways, going through solid rock for most of their length, were less subject to damage from roof pressure. In addition they were big and solid enough to allow 100 HP diesel locomotives hauling trains of three ton capacity mine cars at some speed and safety. Llanharan was the first colliery in Wales to use Horizon Mining, and was very efficient at cutting the tunnels. We advanced two yards per shift, six yards per day. Really good going.

I was on a horizon only 100 yards below the surface when we blasted into an old roadway. There was no indication on the plans of old workings. They must have been very old. I took a look inside. The timber supports were old fashioned collar and pair. There was a piece of chain on the floor similar to the chains little boys put around their waists in Victorian times to haul sledges of coal. The air in the roadway was sweet as a nut, and flowing! When I got to the surface I spoke to the manager about it. If the air was flowing it must be going somewhere. He allowed me to check it out, but to keep an eye on the roof and take a canary with me.

"Universal Pit, Senghenydd.
The Canary that was carried down the Mine
to test the air"

Canaries are kept in coal mines to test for carbon
monoxide. This gas is invisible, has no smell and is highly
toxic. It changes the blood to carboxihaemaglobin. It doesn't
have to be a canary. Any small warm blooded creature would
feel the effects of CO before a grown man would. You could

use a mouse, but you wouldn't notice if it died. A canary would fall off its perch. You could use a small woman, and when she'd stopped talking you'd know she had detected the gas.

I walked down the old roadway. It was in good condition. After 50 yards or so I came to a place where the roadway began to incline upwards. There was a broken brattice cloth door there. To my left were two inclines going upwards, and I noticed that both had collapsed not far from the junction. To my right was a rough wooden table and a bench. On the table was a letter, held down by a piece of coal.

The letter was written in pencil and read as follows:

> My own darling wife and sweetheart I am the only one left. They are all gone. There was a big explosion and a fall of roof. My leg is broke and I am very weak. I only got an inch of candle left, then I will be in the dark. But I will try to follow the direction of the air to the surface. I am sure I can make it, and we can celebrate my 23d birthday together. But if I fail, my love, I hope somebody will give you this letter, so you will know that at the last I was thinking of you.
>
> your ever loving husband Dai.

The roadway onward was much smaller than before. I realised that it had never been used for men or for hauling coal. It was merely a ventilation incline. I was experiencing natural ventilation.

Natural ventilation is a phenomenon used a lot by coal miners in the old days. If the exit is at a higher altitude than the entrance the difference in atmospheric pressure induces a flow of air - natural ventilation. It's the chimney principle. I was bent double going up the steep incline. I was a fit young man and I found it hard going. What must it have been like for a weakened man with a broken leg, in absolute disorientating darkness? I feared the worst. I expected to come across a bundle of bones on the floor.

After a while I saw a smudge of light far ahead. I turned off my cap lamp, shook out my flame lamp and sat in the dark looking at that smudge of light. I imagined what young Dai must have thought. I was the same age, 22, and felt an affinity towards him. "Go on, Dai," I was thinking, "You can do it."

I was talking to him, urging him on over many decades. Dai would have had no idea of the time of day. Perhaps he was resting in despair just where I was sitting, when the new dawn showed him the smudge of light I could see. Maybe that gave him the hope to struggle on.

I relit my cap lamp and flame lamp. The canary greeted the light with a song, and with dread in my heart I continued my struggle up the slope. I found no bones. I broke out onto the side of the mountain and the blessed sunshine. I laughed. Dai must have made it.

I reported to the manager, and he decided to seal off the roadway at both ends. But I was interested in finding out more. I went to the Glamorgan Gazette to look at old newspapers. I had the help of a journalist who thought there might be a story in it. I had to guess the date. I knew it was before 1900 and probably after 1800.

It took a bit of digging, then I found a headline in August 1824. "Nine men killed in Pant tragedy". The paper gave the full story.

There had been an explosion in Pant Colliery, a small private mine, and all nine men and boys had been killed. A rescue party had been driven back by carbon monoxide, but reported that the two headings leading to the pillar and stall workings had completely collapsed and there was no sign of life.

The coroner took expert advice and concluded that the brattice door at the bottom of the workings, leading air up to the workplace was either damaged or had been left open. A small amount of methane, lighter than air, had accumulated at the top and reached an explosive state of around ten per cent methane. 15 per cent and there would not have been enough oxygen to support combustion, under 5 per cent not enough methane to burn. Nine per cent, deadly. A candle had set off a gas explosion which raised a cloud of coal dust which itself exploded and raised another cloud of coal dust........ Not only did the explosions knock out all the timber supports, causing a fall of roof. The shortage of oxygen caused incomplete combustion, resulting in the production of carbon monoxide. No-one could have survived. The coroner made recommendations that no mining should be allowed unless supervised by competent officials, but like all coroner's recommendations of the time it was ignored.

The following week's paper had features on some of the victims' families. The youngest victim was ten year old Ambrose White. He died with his father Richard and left a widow with two girls to bring up.

The next week had a headline "Miracle escape of Brynna miner". It went on: "22 year old David John Trump of 40 Southall Street, Brynna escaped from the inferno of Pant Colliery." Wow! Not only was Dai the same age as me, he was living in the house where I was born!

Dai had been at the top of the workings when he felt there was something wrong with the ventilation. He walked down the incline to have a look at the brattice door. He had almost reached the bottom when the explosion occurred.

He was knocked to the floor and buried in a fall of roof. Because he was lying on the ground he escaped the carbon monoxide, which is lighter than air. He must have been lying there unconscious when the rescue men came in. When he recovered his senses he managed to free himself from the broken roof and, in the dark, feel his way to the junction, where he found by touch a candle on the table and lit it. He then started his long journey out. When he reached the surface he surprised a courting couple frolicking on the mountainside. The strong young farmer put Dai on his back and carried him down, while the girl ran down with the good news.

Dai was so lauded for his fortitude that they raised money for him in a smoking concert in the Eagle, with a grand draw and a collection which came to £140. Dai said he would never go down a pit again, and neither would any son of his. With the money he and his wife moved to Scotland and started a new life there.

I have often wondered how the history of the world might have been changed if David John Trump had not survived his ordeal.

Burnished in the Brynna Sun

After that time lot of good comes with growing old. But there is downside. You become less adventurous and more careful. And, sadly, there is no-one around to remember you in the April of your prime, when you could run like the wind, when you were utterly fearless, in the open, pointing your wooden machine gun at German bombers droning overhead; when you had aspersions of becoming a film star or owning a motor car.

I suppose it's worse for ladies. Men's lined features look rugged. Men don't mind if they can't easily go shopping. Old men can still go banging into a pub on their own. Old ladies feel Less able to do so. Remember that old lady in the wheelchair you saw in the garden centre? Let's call her Emma. Once she was 17 year old Emma, beautiful and in love for the first time with a dashing young cavalry officer. Did he break her heart? Was he a cad or did they marry and live happily ever after? No-one knows, no-one cares. No-one can remember her pink cheeks and sparkling eyes.

I knew an Emma. I knew her in the Brynn's before the old king died. She was nearly 100 years old. I was a little kid with a lot of blonde curly hair and blue eyes, who was invited to functions a a sort of mascot, a good luck charm, a decoration. I was the Kate Moss of the Brynn's. No party was complete unless I was there.

She had a big house just outside the Brynna on the way to Llanharan. She was holding a Christening party for her great grand-daughter. Both the old lady and the baby were named Emma. She lived in a different world to most of us.

She had a car but had never driven one. She said the goggles didn't suit her. She had a mechanic to drive her about.

Apart from those two and me there were three generations in between, her surviving children and most of her grand children and great grandchildren. They were all chatting away, as always on family gatherings, about what they all got up to in their younger days. "Do you remember when.....? "I'll never forget when...."

No-one talked about the old lady's past because no-one was alive who could remark upon it. She was just a dignified old lady sitting in a chair listening to the excited conversations of her descendants. She was like a candle alone on a shelf. i was standing by her chair, eating the sandwiches on her plate. She didn't seem to mind. We were all in what they called a summer house, but I suppose now we would call it a conservatory.

Her oldest grandson came to talk to her. He had sported some repairs needed to the summer house. "The old place is getting a bit run down, grandmother" he said, "We should do something about it."

The old lady said, " it's not so old. I remember it being built. Before it was built all this was a pleasure garden. My father had made it. It had steps from the house into the garden, and the garden had lawns and bushes, flowers and sweet smelling herbs everywhere, and a cherry tree. In the spring the cherry tree had lovely blossom and in the summer it produced a lot of fruit. There was a swing hanging between two other trees."

"I recall when I was about eight, sitting on the swing in the garden. I met your grandfather for the first time. He had come to see my father on business and afterwards he came bounding down the steps towards me. He was tall and straight and handsome, and he had a wicked black moustache. I remember as it were yesterday."

She sighed. "The pleasure garden was such an oasis of peace.there was no noise of traffic, no radios. Only the sound of doves coo-ing in the dovecote, of the birds in the trees and the breezes rustling the leaves. Butterflies dried their wings in the sunshine and the sweetest of smells came from the rose garden and the banks of flowers around me. It was Heavenly."

"I had a lot of golden curls at that time, just like young John here." She patted my head. "He said to me, 'Hello young lady, sitting here burnished by the Brynn's sun'. I think I fell in love with him at that instant. I watched his lips under that black moustache, forming the words, 'burnished by the Brynna sun.'. I said to him, "push me, push me on the swing." He had a deep laugh, and as he pushed I called to him, 'higher, higher'. I flew higher than the trees, I imagined, until I begged him to stop. He pretended to be exhausted".

"There were two fat blackbirds under the cherry tree, feasting on the fallen fruit, and he said, 'Why should they get all the fun?'. He collected cherries off the tree and put them in my hand. They were warm against my palm. We are the cherries, our first meal together."

"He came again the next day, then went away. But he came back the following summer, and the summer afterwards. I lived for those summer visits. I agonised over what I should wear, nothing too severe, and certainly nothing too young. After eight years of summer visits he asked my father for my hand in marriage."

"My father said, 'First I will build a fine summerhouse, and we will use it for your wedding feast'. This is the summer house that he built for me. Now, like me, it is getting old. But I have had the pleasure of nursing my great grand daughter, and they have been kind enough to name her after me." She lapsed into silence."

Her grandson said, " Dear Granny, why don't we take down the old summer house? I will rebuild your pleasure garden for you, as it was when you were a child. Maybe young Emma there will sit on the swing and maybe she will meet her husband there."

The old lady stirred and looked at him. She put her frail hand out to him and touched his cheek lovingly. "Ah!" she said, "You are a dreamer, just like your grandfather".

The Butcher of Brynna

Alfie Bird kept the butcher's shop in William Street. He wasn't Welsh. His mother was Irish and his father was English. I don't know how he landed up in the Brynna. He said he got on the wrong bus in Gloucester. Gloucester was to the road network what Crewe was to the rail network.

Alfie was of generous proportions and of an amiable disposition. In the bad times, during the general strike and the following depression, he'd taken the hit with his customers, allowing credit, not knowing if he'd ever get it back.

Even though life was a little easier in the mid 1930s Brynna was not an affluent society. Much of what he offered was of the cheaper variety.

Nevertheless his window was a joy to behold. Rabbits were cheap and plentiful. Farmers considered them pests. They shot them and sold them to the butcher for coppers. Rabbits are easy to skin, like shelling peas. They hung in his windows in all their naked glory. When a customer brought a child into the shop Alfie would give the child a lucky rabbit's foot for luck. Tripe and chitterlings glistened invitingly. His sausages were plump and meaty, and his faggots sat in spicy juice in earthenware containers. He made his own brawn and sold pork dripping. The pork fat was silvery and with the shiny brown jelly below it made a very tasty spread. It was Dad's favourite in his Tommy box at work.

He had the better cuts of meat as well. He bought in whole Welsh lambs. Mr Davies, the chapel superintendent, kept pigs, and slaughtered them on a bench outside his bakehouse in our back lane, to the fascination of the small boys watching. He'd slit the pig's throat and after it stopped squealing hang it up in his bakehouse, bring buckets of hot water to shave it then pass it to Alfie Bird to butcher it and sell it.

Some he would sell fresh, but some he would salt and hang from hooks in his ceiling. There were salted hams hanging there, and sides of salted bacon. The bacon was mostly fat, with just a little red meat.

You may enthuse about the full English breakfast, but it doesn't measure up to the full Welsh breakfast. My mouth waters still, after all these years, at the thought of it. Two rashers of very thick, very salty bacon sizzling in the pan, with an egg fried in butter, black pudding and fried bread. Breakfast fit for a king!

His shin beef was perfect for Cawl, a dish made with root vegetables cooked over two days, with stars floating on the top. Brawn, if you could forget what it was made of, was a tasty treat. He sold duck eggs as well, big blue eggs just right for a birthday treat. We didn't always buy them there. When ducks get broody in the spring they aim to escape from their owner's pen and make a secret nest out in the wilds where they can incubate their eggs and bring up a family. The owners didn't actually discourage this because it increased their duck flock. But Brynna boys also knew about it and would search out the duck nests and take the eggs.

We in the Brynna were living very well and Alfie Bird was also doing well. In 1939 he bought a new Jaguar motor car, but Mr Hitler poked his nose into our affairs and Alfie couldn't get any petrol coupons. After the war he was driving a practically new 1939 Jaguar!

It was a Saturday night in early June. Alfie Bird was a contented man. He'd had a pretty good week. Most of his stock had been sold and he was expecting a delivery on

Monday. He had cleared all the meat from the window and put it in the walk-in fridge at the back of the shop. As he swept the sawdust from his shop he thought of his immediate plans.

He had saved a very nice piece of beef for his dinner the following day. His wife Rosie would cook it with Yorkshire pudding and the vegetables he would collect from his allotment on Sunday morning. He would dig his first new potatoes of the year, cut a nice Savoy cabbage, pick some fresh young broad beans and collect carrots, the second thinning, the sweetest of all carrots, all covered with Rosie's gravy. Perfect.

But before dinner, up to the Eagle for a drink. Sunday lunch time is the most sophisticated drinking of all. No-one is tired. No-one is drunk. A couple of pints, home for dinner, then pack off the kids to Sunday School and enjoy a relaxing afternoon with Rosie. He sucked his teeth in anticipation.

The smile was still on his face when Mrs Flynn burst into the shop. Mrs Flynn was the only Irish lady in the Brynna. She looked like Tommy Farr, big shoulders, short neck:. She was on a mission. "Mr Bird, Mr Bird, I'm having four people for dinner tomorrow. Would you ever have a nice chicken for me?"

He liked Mrs Flynn. He always affected an Irish accent when he spoke to her. "Is it yourself, Mrs Flynn? I'll just go to my old fridge and see what I've got there."

There was just one chicken in the fridge, and it wasn't looking too special. He knocked the chicken into shape and put it on the counter. "There you are Mrs Flynn. That'll be £2 so it will. You'll be putting your auld potatoes and onion stuffing in there will you not?"

She said, "Mr Bird, I'm having FOUR people for dinner

tomorrow. That chicken is nowhere near big enough. Do you have a bigger one?"

"I'll go and have a look". He picked up the chicken, took it back to the fridge. He spread out its wings. He pulled on the legs. He blew down its neck. He took it back out and put it on the counter. "There you are Mrs Flynn, £3."

She said, "Mr Bird, Mr Bird, you've saved my life. I'll take both of them."

The Sad Story

Mr Brown, my English teacher, was a gem. He gave us pupils the lifelong joy of love of the English language. He was short and plump and nondescript in appearance, but he had the gift of making fictional characters come alive. Even the "difficult" authors such as Chaucer and Shakespeare fascinated us boys. We laughed with the Wife of Bath, we wept with Malvolio, we shrugged with Shylock.

He introduced us to Thackeray and Thomas Hardy, H.G.Wells and Mark Twain, Conan Doyle and John Dunne, and the delightful desperado Christopher Marlowe, (Come live with me and be my love), killed by a knife in the eye at the age of 29 in Deptford. All these and the great poets he brought to us. In the last lesson of each term he read us a story, with all the actions, like an actor on a stage. We sat in silence, entranced.

He gave us projects. "Write a story" he said, "Give me a fictional story". He gave us different themes. My job was to write a sad story.

I didn't know much about sadness. I could relate incidents which were sad, but I needed a story that was sad all the way through. All my life I found that my best ideas came when I was physically active, such as when I was mowing a lawn or felling a mighty oak tree. So I took my football and went down to the park seeking inspiration.

I found Miss Bull. She was sitting on a bench in the sun, reading a book. She was wearing a navy blue suit, a white blouse and sensible shoes, with leather gloves, a pearl necklace and a hat. Miss Bull was very old. Miss Bull had been my teacher in infant school. She is best remembered for her propensity to blush furiously, head and neck, whenever a man came into her classroom. It didn't matter if it was the Head Master, a man from the Ministry or the Truant Officer. Miss Bull blushed furiously.

I greeted her, asked her how she was. She was now retired, living quietly. She was interested to know how I was getting on. I told her I was in the express stream at Grammar School and I had a problem. I had to find a sad story. She said, "I'll tell you a sad story you can use if you like."

"I was one of five girls in a well off family. I realise now how thoughtless rich children can be, how little we cared for people worse off than ourselves. We had a domestic called Daisy. We called her Daze for short and for fun. We took advantage of her. We expected her to be at our beck and call, taking her away from her paid work. She wasn't a full time domestic. She came in two or three days a week. She had other houses she looked after as well as ours."

"With all those children there was a lot of washing and ironing. Daisy was an expert ironer. Shed have two irons on the fire. Her ironing board was placed on the sideboard at one end and on a chair back at the other. It was covered with a scorched old blanket. When she ironed our skirts she would sprinkle the skirt with water and roll it up. When all the skirts were rolled she would take the first one, unroll It, lift one end of the ironing board and slip the skirt over it. She would test the iron for heat by holding it close to her cheek. Some women tested by spitting on the iron to see if it sizzled, but not our Daze. She was too refined for that. When she was finished the skirt was beautifully ironed and put on a skirt hanger in the airing cupboard."

"Mother and Daze would stretch sheets together. There would be a huge pile of bed sheets every wash day. They had a system. They stood apart, feet braced, and pulled the sheet tight. We watched in the hope that one of them slipped and they fell on their backs, but that never happened. There was that little dance when they approached each other to fold the sheet, and the dance back to stretch again. So, steadily, the jumbled pile of sheets decreased in size, while the pile of stretched sheets increased in size."

"She worked furiously on the mangle. As she turned the wooden wheels by the steel handle she would sing a song for us:

> Oh my mother had a mangle
>
> And she turned it by the handle
>
> And when its on full power
>
> It does forty shirts an hour
>
> Did you ever see, did you ever see
>
> Did you ever see such a funny thing before"

"Daisy had a sweetheart named Asquith. He had a little watch and clock business in the front room of his house in William Street. We took advantage of him too. Because he loved Daisy he was keen to please us. He spent a lot of time making little clockwork toys for us, instead of earning money for himself. He lived very frugally, although we didnt know that. I asked him to make a steam engine for me, powered by methylated spirits. I would fill the tank with the meths, light the wick, and as the water boiled it would turn a little brass wheel. It wasn't useful for anything, except to amuse me, and it must have taken him a lot of time to make it. I have it still, but I don't play with it any more. It makes me sad to remember."

" Mother was good to Daisy. She treated her more like a friend than a domestic. She gave a party to celebrate the twenty-fifth anniversary of Daisy's engagement to Asquith. Asquith brought mother a bunch of shop-bought flowers, quite an expense for him."

" It was probably the happiest day of poor Daisys life. She and her sweetheart were treated like honoured guests in a big house. They were served with their tea by us children, for once giving something back to them for all they had given us throughout our childhood."

" Asquith was 55 then, Daisy about five years younger. I didn't know if Asquith was his Christian name or his surname. That shows how little I cared about him". She paused. I had never known Miss Bull to be so garrulous. Here she was, pouring out her spinster heart to me, a schoolboy.

" You were born at the right time, John. You are young and strong. Education is free to you. You can even go to university if you want to. Health care is easily available to you. That nice Mr Attlee is bringing a bright new dawn to the working class."

" For poor old Daisy and Asquith it was different. They had struggled mightily for all their lives, with little reward. They were no nearer being able to get married now than when they became engaged a quarter of a century before. The Brynna wasn't really prosperous enough to support a watch and clock shop. Where you have hope and opportunity they had despair and poverty. Work was dropping off for Asquith, and he was becoming more unwell. We girls didnt notice that."

" A couple of years after the party, one Wednesday, Daisy didn't come to work. I asked mother where Daisy was. Was she ill? No said mother,

Asquith died. Today is his funeral."

Miss Bull sat on the park bench, in her leather gloves and pearl necklace. Although I was there,Miss Bull was alone. Her body shook with sobs. Then she died. She just...........
died.

The Twinning

Nowadays it's Scotsmen. They are like fleas. They get everywhere. But in those days, 1937, it was Welshmen who were ubiquitous. Wherever in the British Empire you travelled, Hong Kong, or India, or Singapore, the man in charge was always English. It was the Englishman who went to the fine functions, welcomed visiting royalty, took all the headlines. But invariably the man who did all the work, all the administration, made most of the decisions was the anonymous Welshman one tier below him.

It was the time when a less anonymous Welshman, Tommy Farr, made headlines around the world by going the distance with world heavyweight boxing champion Joe Louis. It was the Tonypandy Terror v. the Brown Bomber, the accidental boxer. Joe's mother had considered music to be the only way out of poverty for her boy, and bought him a violin. On his way to his first violin lesson he passed a boxing gym.....

It was the first time Joe Louis had failed to finish off a contender for his title inside fifteen rounds. And it was a close run thing. Most Welshmen thought Tommy Farr had done enough to take the title. My uncle Tim, who lived next door to us in the Brynna, although largely unschooled, had built a wireless with all the valves etc. He could "Get America" on it. A number of men stayed up until three o'clock in the morning in Tim's house to listen to the fight. I wanted to stay up as well. Dad was willing, but Mam thought that at five years old it was well past my bed time. I believe the commentary on the wireless was barely discernable, but it was live and it was exciting. Tommy Farr was a hero.

I met him when I was working in London 35 years later. I saw him standing alone at the end of a tube platform. I approached him, I said "Hello champ". He nodded graciously. I asked if there was anything I could do to help him, but he was OK. He was huge. His shoulders were as thick as mine were wide. Even at 70 plus he was frightening just standing there. I knew he could have killed me with one punch. The upshot was that we all felt proud and important. Tommy Farr wasn't from the Brynna, but he wasn't so far away that we couldn't claim him for our own.

Mr McAndrew, Public Speaker, Pillar of the Community and Person of Note felt that the Brynna should spread its wings a little, become known internationally. Mr McAndrew was ahead of his time, and he dreamed up a scheme to be associated with a foreign town. His research brought up Braunau, a little town in Austria just on the German border, and so similar in name to the Brynna. It was a late medieval town with two churches. Brynna had one church and one chapel. The Emperor Franz Joseph had visited Braunau in 1903. Our own dear King and Queen had passed Brynna in a train quite recently. All this was enough to persuade Mr McAndrew to suggest to the authorities in Braunau that we should set up what we now call Twinning.

Mr McAndrew called a public meeting and set up a small working party. Dad was persuaded to be part of it. Mr McAndrew was very assiduous. He had done his homework in the public library in Pontypridd. He had written to the Home Office in London, which had forwarded his letter to the appropriate office, which welcomed his proposal to improve international relations. It resulted in the offer of a small grant to take Mr McAndrew, as the Most Important Person in the Brynna to Braunau with a German speaking civil servant to meet the Most Important Person in Braunau.

The public meeting thoroughly endorsed Mr McAndrew's proposal and wished him well on his visit to Austria. They anticipated that there would be a return visit, and Dad was given the job of orchestrating that. The Eagle didn't have suitable bedrooms, so he proposed approaching Lady Blandy Jenkins in Llanharan to host the visitors. However, he held fire until he had made investigations.

Mr McAndrew took a train to London and, accompanied by the civil servant Mr Oliver Cooke, took a train to Harwich then a boat to the Hook of Holland. It was a long journey to Braunau, where they had been booked into the Gasthaus Pommer on Salzburger Verstadt. My Cooke was ambivalent about his job. He spent the journey coaching Mr McAndrew on Austrian/German customs and taught him a few useful phrases in German such as "please" and "thank you" and "my friend will pay".

The authorities in Braunau had identified the Most Important Person in the town. He had been born in a house on the Salzburger Verstadt, near where Mr McAndrew was berthed, in 1889. He was now living in Berlin, but returned to Braunau specifically to meet Mr McAndrew and extend the hand of friendship to him and, by association, to the Brynna.

The whole ceremony was conducted in German, and Mr Cooke translated for Mr McAndrew when appropriate. Mr McAndrew must have been impressed because immediately on his return he called a meeting of his working party to report progress and plan the next steps. He reported that he had been received with great politeness, that Braunau was a very pretty little town with 16th and 17th century houses and looked prosperous, very suitable for Twinning with the Brynna. The authorities had given him a gift of a Junghaus mantle clock, which he treasured, and Mr Cooke had been greatly encouraged by the entente cordiale. He had thanked Mr McAndrew warmly for his initiative and said he hoped the proposal would be developed and strengthened over the coming months and years. My McAndrew proposed that they should pursue the Twinning process vigorously. Dad had been doing his own bit of research. He said there was a need to exercise a bit of caution before falling into the arms of the people of Braunau. He asked Mr McAndrew if he had got the name of the Braunau VIP and Mr McAndrew said he had not, he had always been addressed by his title, in German, which he didn't understand. Dad then asked, "Did he have a little black moustache, like Charlie Chaplin?"

Mr McAndrew thought that he might have.

Dad said, " I think you'll find, Mr Chairman, that his first name was Adolf and his surname was Hitler".

The Three Periods

If you take away family matters there are three character forming periods in my life. The two decades since the year 2000 is only a small portion of man's history, but it brought technical developments which changed the world to an extraordinary degree. So much so that young people wonder how anybody ever managed in the 1990s.

We now have tweeting and Netflix, You Tube and social media, Fitbit and apps galore and Zoom, which although imperfect brought some sanity into the closed world of the lockdown of 2020. And we have the miracle of the Covid vaccine.

Then there is the I-phone. That which we cannot live without, that which we have to consult at all times in case we miss something important. It is, of course, wonderful that we can discover in a moment the live scores of any cricket match anywhere in the world. But we've become addicted to it, enslaved by it, right across the age range. If you asked an old lady in 2000 how to cook a piece of beef she would have told you. If you ask an old lady the same question today she'd consult her I phone and give you the torment of choosing which of 20 ways to cook beef, none of which she has tried herself.

We haven't had such a fundamental shake-up of our lives since Harold Wilson was Prime Minister. He was an academic genius, the youngest Oxford don of the century at the age of 21. In his four spells as Prime Minister he visited upon us the four modern Horsemen of the Apocalypse.

He relaxed the law on divorce. Previously very few people were divorced because it was so difficult to arrange. Married couples arrived at rocky patches in their marriage and had to find a way through them. Children grew up in a stable family and couples lived together "till death did them part". There is no privilege more precious than to care for a soul-mate for fifty or sixty years, no greater satisfaction. Now most couples never reach that Nirvana. Now almost all children have friends whose parents are divorced. It's the norm. And Harold Wilson caused it.

It was Harold Wilson who relaxed the law on censorship. Now words once heard only in coal mines and shipyards are common place. Comedians use them to raise a laugh. Playwrights use them because it reflects life as it is today. Footballers on TV use them casually and commentators have to apologise in case viewers heard the naughty words. For many people it is still offensive, and we can thank Harold Wilson for that.

It was Harold Wilson who set up David Steele to look at the vexed question of abortion rights. There are strongly held views on both sides of this question, and David Steele, an honourable man, advised the Prime Minister that abortion should be allowed in exceptional cases, e.g. when the life of the mother was at risk and this should be certified by two doctors. But of course it has become abortion on demand, for the most frivolous of reasons, and thousands of helpless babies are killed every year by doctors who swear when they graduate to "do no harm". The super-intelligent Wilson did not foresee that.

It was Harold Wilson who repealed the law against homosexuality. It is true that something had to be done to right this wrong, but there might have been a better way of doing it. There are good points and bad points, and it's not clear if the good points outweigh the bad points. Like opinions on, say, capital punishment and Brexit, there are honest, intelligent people who have opposing views.

Before all this the world was quite a different place. Few people are old enough to remember the days before Harold Wilson. Few can remember the time when we were shocked by the language of Rhett Butler in Gone with the Wind, saying, " Frankly my dear, I don't give a damn."

Children used to go to the Saturday matinee in Llanharan cinema, at a cost of three pence, to see cowboy serials. The cheap seats were wooden benches. The boys were kept on one side of the aisle, the girls on the other. During gunfights there was rapt attention. When love scenes came on the boys erupted, and the manager would run maniacally down the aisle shouting at us.

Mam and Dad used to go at different times, sitting in the one and nines (costing one shilling and ninepence). There was nothing offensive in the films, but the world was slowly changing. Jane Russell, in The Outlaw, lay half exposed in a haystack, and I'll never forget the day I was in the cinema in Pencoed with Mam watching the film Shaft, and hearing the naughtiest word of all. I was so embarrassed! But I think it was the episode with the chicken that put an end to their cinema going.

No-Good-Boyo had gone to Spain to fight in the International Brigade against Franco. In spite of (or because of) being brought up in the Brynna, he was a sensitive soul, and having witnessed the horrors of that brutal campaign, returned home rather more deranged than when he went to Spain.

He loved his little dog, and when it died he was inconsolable. Then he found a chicken limping along the road in Brynna. For him it was like the road to Damascus.

The chicken had hurt its foot. No-Good-Boyo took it home and took care of it. Before long he had adopted it as a pet. They were inseparable. He took it for walks. He took it on the bus to the sea-side. He bought it treats. It was the most pampered chicken, certainly in the Brynna, and possibly in the world.

He took it to the cinema, where Mam and Dad were enjoying a rare outing. The usherette said to No-Good-Boyo "You can't bring that chicken in here." No-Good-Boyo was accustomed to people rejecting his chicken. He didn't argue. He just went outside, stuffed the chicken down his trousers and went back in and bought a ticket. He sat next to Mam, so she was sandwiched between him and Dad.

After a while the chicken began to get restless. No-Good-Boyo undid the buttons on his fly so that the chicken could poke his head out, have a look around. In the darkness of the cinema Mam couldn't see clearly, but she whispered to Dad, "I think the man next to me is exposing himself to me." Dad recognised No-Good-Boyo. It put him in a bit of a dilemma. No-Good-Boyo was already on a yellow card with the police, and Dad didn't want to cause a fuss and see him arrested and charged with indecent behaviour.

He said, "Pay no attention, Hild, when you've seen one you've seen them all."

Mam said, " Yes, but this one is eating my crisps."

The Adventures of Tommy Yorke

By rights the Top Field should be mine. It had belonged to my maternal grandfather. He had four daughters who had lots of children and two sons who had none acknowledged. My grandfather died intestate and as the oldest grandson I am the nearest thing to a son and heir. If the lawyers got hold of it they would share it out amongst his numerous descendants, and we would all get about a square yard each.

My grandfather got the field in a queer way. He was renting it from Mr West as a smallholding, trying and failing to earn a living for him and his bride Rosie Fields. Life was hard, made harder by a quarrel with neighbour Mr Lastella over a right of way. Going to the lawyers was expensive and solved nothing. He got into arrears with the rent and Rosie became grumpy. He decided to take decisive action and earn a fortune in America.

He dressed in his best clothes, fancy waistcoat, Dai cap, moleskin trousers with the Yorkes. He was the only man in the village to wear Yorkes. His nickname was Tommy Yorke. Yorkes are leather shoelaces tied around the trouser legs just below the knee. I dont know why. I think it may be a Prussian fashion. He hadnt walked far before he came across a man much more worse off than himself. The beggar persuaded my grandfather to give him five shillings and to change clothes with him. The well dressed beggar went one way, my poorly dressed grandfather went the other.

The beggar reached the Brynna and walked into the contentious right of way. In the dark, Mr Lastella thought it was Tommy Yorke. "Get out of here you scoundrel" he cried, and hit him with a cudgel. He hit him so hard he killed him, and with the help of his brothers carried him into Brynna Wood and buried him in a shallow grave.

Tommy Yorke travelled on, reached America and got a job in a canning factory in Chicago. The factory had a cheerful slogan on the wall "We eat all we can and what we cant we can". It wasn't a cheerful job. The factory had a chain lift, going from floor level to the roof. Live pigs arrived at the bottom of the chain lift and the back legs hog-tied. The pig was hoisted onto the ever moving chain lift and hauled into the air. My grandfather was on a platform six feet off the ground. As the pig went past him he stabbed it in the throat with a knife. By the time the pig reached the roof it had bled out, and was processed on its way back to ground level, leaving the factory as cans of pork meat. Grandfather was spending ten hours a day stabbing pigs at the rate of two a minute. He could have done it in his sleep.

The pay was poor, but he could take home an allowance of cans of pork every day. He soon tired of pork. His appetite was poor, and his health suffered. He became pale, gaunt, emaciated, something of the spectral about him. The concrete canyons of Chicago shut him off from the sunshine, when the sun was shining in that Windy City. He longed for the green pastures of the Brynna. He began to think of his smallholding with affection, and even fell in love again with Rosie. He put together some money with the help of friends and bought a ticket on a steamer to Bristol, two years after he had left it.

As he landed in Bristol some boys collecting acorns in Brynna Wood discovered the body of the beggar man. The body was not recognisable, but Tommy Yorkes clothes were. Rosie was able to put an end to that chapter of her life, and Mr Lastella, who had always fancied Rosie, saw his chance to move in.

Meanwhile Tommy Yorke set off to walk home. He arrived in the Brynna after dark, even thinner and paler than when he had left America. When he got to his house he saw his best clothes hanging on the washing line. Rosie had been given the clothes by the police and had given them a good wash. "Well done Rosie girl" he thought to himself, and dressed himself in his finery, trademark Yorkes and all.

When he went into his house he found Rosie and Mr Lastella perched like two lovebirds on the organ bench, playing a four-handed. When they saw Tommy they screamed and ran out of the house, leading Tommy to think that there was something going on.

He went next door where there was a party in full swing. He stopped the jollification in its tracks. They all fled the house as if the Devil himself was after them. Tommy Yorke was thinking that was a strange welcome home for any traveller. He didnt want hugs and kisses, but a "Good to see you" would have been nice. He decided to go and see his landlord Mr West to make his peace and reclaim the Top Field.

Nobody locked their doors in the Brynna at that time, and he walked in to find Mr and Mrs West at supper. "Ive come back" said Tommy, " to settle up all I owe you and take over the Top Field again. I cant give you the money right now, but give me a little time and I'll square it with you".

Mr West was trapped behind his kitchen table. He couldn't run out. "I wont take your money, Tommy" he said, " I forgive all your debts to me".

"Well" said Tommy, " That's the first welcome words Ive heard since I came back, and I thank you for your kind offer. Now all I would ask is for a little time, if it pleases you, to pay my future rent".

Mr West, looking green about the gills, demurred again. "I wouldn't dream of taking any money from you for the future rents. In fact Ill give you a writ to let you have the field free of rent for 999 years."

So it happened. Mr West that very evening drew up a proper legal writ, forgiving Tommy all his current debts and giving him the Top Field free of all let or hindrance, rent free for the next 999 years. It was full of "whatsoevers" and "notwithstandings" and properly signed by Mr West, witnessed by Mrs West, countersigned by Thomas Evans Esquire, and dated.

I found the writ in Mam's papers after she died, amongst her birth certificate, marriage certificate etc. So I reckon that Tommy Yorke must have intended the Top Field to come to me, and passed the writ onto his eldest daughter to pass on to his own favourite grandson.

Or should I pass it on to my own great grandson Alfie? He has Tommy Yorke's DNA, passed down over five generations. Tommy Yorke had the heart of a lion. Maybe Alfie will inherit his courage and his luck as well.

Other books by John Hiett

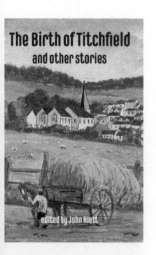

The Birth of Titchfield and Other Stories

This collection of short stories by several authors, draws upon tales from Titchfield's past.

ISBN: 978-1-909054-50-9 (paperback)
ISBN: 978-1-909054-51-6 (hardcover)

A Touch of Purple

The village of Titchfield in Hampshire has various royal connections, extending over time from the Saxon kings to James II, and include one royal wedding. John Hiett has assembled the work of several historians to create this book.

ISBN: 978-1-909054-63-9

Lightning Source UK Ltd.
Milton Keynes UK
UKHW022151200221
378988UK00006B/107

9 781909 054738